Partition

The Price of Quebec's
Independence

PARTITION

The Price of Quebec's Independence

A Realistic Look at the Possibility of Quebec
Separating From Canada and Becoming an
Independent State.

William F. Shaw and Lionel Albert

Foreword by Eugene Forsey

Thornhill Publishing
Montreal

Graphics by Rik Rok

Printed and bound in Canada.
80 81 82 83 10 9 8 7 6 5 4 3 2 1

Thornhill Publishing,
175 Stillview Road, Suite 260,
Pointe Claire, P.Q. H9R 4S3 Canada
ISBN 0-9690325-0-1

also do not want their children to grow up ignorant of, or ill-equipped in, the predominant language of North America, and handicapped economically for the rest of their lives. These people, like the Italian, Greek and other "immigrant" communities in Quebec, have already been deprived of their freeedom of choice in the education of their children, and would certainly not regain it in an independent Quebec. "If this shall be done in the green tree," before independence, "what shall be done in the dry," after?

I have very personal reasons for feeling passionate about the fate of the English-speaking minority in Quebec. I belonged to it for sixteen years. Two of my grandparents and four of my great-grandparents belonged to it. My roots in Quebec go back well over a hundred years. I was brought up in the household of my maternal grandfather, who, born and brought up in Quebec City, came to live in Ottawa only when it became the capital of first, the pre-Confederation Province of Canada, then of the Dominion. (He was an official first, of the Legislative Assembly of the Province of Canada, then of the House of Commons of the Dominion, and when his employer moved, he, perforce, moved too.) Born in Newfoundland, I have lived nearly all my life in, or on the edge of, Quebec; and from my earliest years Montreal, where we had many relations and friends, not Toronto, where we had few, was the big city where we went shopping and visiting. Even before I went to live there, Montreal was almost as much my home as Ottawa.

Two features of the present situation of the Quebec English-speaking minority appal me.

The first is the degree to which many of its "leaders" (what are sometimes called its "natural" or "traditional" leaders), and some of its "intellectuals", seem ready to accept a status of second class citizens. I am tired of these Dukes of Plaza Toro, who lead their regiment from behind ("they find it less exciting," or perhaps less costly). I am tired of "these gentle warblers of the grove, these moderate Whigs and temperate statesmen," as Lord Chatham called the Rockingham Whigs. I am frightened by their willingness to lie down on their backs with all four feet in the air. I am heartened by the vigour with which Dr. Shaw, Mr. Albert and their friends have been battling to defend the rights of their fellow-citizens.

Foreword

by the Honourable Eugene Forsey

When Dr. Shaw asked me to write a foreword to this book, I accepted at once, with enthusiasm, and that, for several reasons.

First, in the whole discussion of Quebec independence, the separatists have too often been allowed to define the basis, the terms, the vocabulary and the limits of the debate. This has given them a marked, and quite undeserved, advantage. It is high time someone spoke out loud and clear to challenge the bland, often insolent, assumptions which have been foisted on a gullible public. This book challenges a series of those assumptions.

Second, the debate has too often taken place in a great "cloud of unknowing" and fairy-tales. That cloud this book penetrates, those fairy-tales it shows up for the imaginative nonsense they are. Its historical research has been thorough, and the results are impressive.

Third, I am deeply concerned by what separatism would do to minorities, in Quebec and in the other provinces.

In Quebec, this means the English-speaking minority. That includes many thousands of people who are not of British origin, but who do not want their children to grow up ignorant of, or ill-equipped in, the prevailing language of almost the whole of this continent north of the Rio Grande. That in an independent Quebec they would be so deprived, Bill 101 is proof. That, so deprived, they would, when they grew up, find their mobility, their chance of getting jobs outside Quebec, their chance of getting ahead, severely restricted, requires no proof but shines like the stars in heaven.

In the other provinces, it is the French-speaking minorities that would suffer. Their position, immensely strengthened by legislation and administration in recent years, notably in Ontario and New Brunswick, where most of them live, would be drastically and tragically weakened.

In the fourth place, I am concerned for those French-Canadians in Quebec (and I suspect they may be many) who

Notes about usage

To make it easy for everybody we shall use the word
"separatist" to describe anyone favouring sovereignty or independence for a French-Canadian state, with or without special
association with the rest of Canada.

Readers unfamiliar with French usage will note that a
Péquiste (adj. *péquiste*) is a partisan of the *Parti Québécois*, a
political party at the provincial level in Quebec which favours a
form of separation called "Sovereignty-Association".

American readers will have to muddle through the fact that
the initials "P.Q." sometimes mean *Parti Québécois* and sometimes "Province of Quebec". They should also note the fact
that one of the differences between Canadian and U.S. federal
structures is that the Canadian Federal government can dis-
allow any law passed by the legislature of a province, within a
year of its passage. Finally, we note that the Seven Years' War
is more familiar to U.S. readers as the "French and Indian
War."

Where established English place-names exist, we use them
— hence *Montreal*, not *Montréal*; *Three Rivers*, not *Trois-
Rivières*; but: *Trois-Pistoles*; *St-Jérôme*.

Acknowledgements

I wish to thank Leslie Roberts, veteran journalist and broadcaster, who encouraged me to move forward with this book, and who has been teacher, advisor, and conscience during its creation.

I also wish to give special thanks to John Robertson, whose personal commitment to freedom and justice motivated me to become involved in the fight for Canada. John made me see that nothing worth having comes without effort and personal sacrifice.

I also wish to thank Olga Dufour and Denise Joanisse, my secretaries, who typed and re-typed the several drafts of the manuscript.

— William F. Shaw

I wish to thank the various members of the Reference staff of the McLennan Library at McGill University, and the staff at the Aegidius Fauteux Annex of the Quebec Provincial Library, for their assistance.

I especially wish to thank Mrs Janet Sader and Mrs Nellie Reiss who are the guardians of the treasures of the Lande Collection at McGill University. Their wise and knowledgeable help was invaluable to one who had not frequented a university library for more years than he cares to remember. I would also like to thank Mrs Carol Marley of the Map Room at the McLennan Library for her prompt and able assistance.

— Lionel Albert

LIST OF ILLUSTRATIONS

LIST OF MAPS

CONTENTS

Grateful acknowledgement is made:

To the Cambridge University Press for permission to quote from *The Later Correspondence of George III*, edited by A. Aspinall

To Les Presses de l'Université de Montréal for permission to quote a passage which appears in Chapter 4 from *L'Accession à la souveraineté et le cas du Québec*, by Jacques Brossard

To Thomas Nelson & Sons (Canada) Ltd for permission to use a map of early settlement in Lower Canada from *An Historical Atlas of Canada*, edited by Lawrence J. Burpee

To Les Éditions de l'Homme Ltée for permission to reproduce the Chart of Association of Quebec-Canada, to copy the historical maps which appear in Chapter 4, and to quote two passages from *L'Option*, by Jean-Pierre Charbonneau and Gilbert Paquette

To McClelland and Stewart Limited, Toronto, as the Canadian publishers of *Quebec: The Revolutionary Age*, by Hilda Neatby and of *Beatty of the C.P.R.*, by D.H. Miller-Barstow, for permission to quote one passage from each book

To the University of Toronto Press for permission to quote from *Fort Timiskaming and the Fur Trade*, by Elain Allan Mitchell

To the Yale University Press for permission to use the insert map of the negotiations of 1755 and to quote a passage from *The Diplomatic History of the Canadian Boundary, 1749-1763*, by Max Savelle

To Les Presses de l'Université Laval for permission to reproduce detail from four maps, and the whole of a fifth map, from *Atlas Historique du Canada français,* edited by Marcel Trudel

To H. M. Public Records Office, Kew, for permission to reproduce a portion of the original of Lord Halifax's letter of September 19, 1763.

We wish to express our appreciation to His Excellency the Apostolic Nuncio, Ottawa, for his generous assistance in supplying the data from which we compiled the figure on Italian participation in the Vatican, which appears on page 48.

To our wives, Cathryn and June

W.F.S. and L.A.

Second, I am even more dismayed by the apparently growing willingness in English-speaking Canada outside Quebec to leave the Quebec English-speaking minority to its fate; to offer it as a reasonable, acceptable and living sacrifice to the preservation of a "Canada" which would be hardly more than a splash on the map with a six-letter label, a pale ghost of the deceased Canadian nation. (One has only to look at the numerous proposals to leave each province to settle its language question as the majority in that province sees fit.)

These people need to be told that there is in Quebec a large, active and deep-rooted English-speaking community. It is close to 900,000 souls: larger than the total population of Nova Scotia, or the combined populations of Newfoundland and Prince Edward Island, or the combined populations of New Brunswick and Prince Edward Island, and nearly as large as the total population of Manitoba or Saskatchewan. In the metropolitan area of Montreal, English is the language most often spoken in the home by about 700,000 people, which is more than the total population of any metropolitan area except Toronto and Vancouver.

This book provides evidence that this English-speaking community has leaders who are not Plaza Toros; who are not prepared to see it made a doormat for, or a living sacrifice to, Quebec French-Canadian nationalism; who do not acknowledge any Herrenvolk; who intend to preserve their rights as Canadian citizens; who, if the worst comes to the worst, will claim their own right to self-determination, their right to take themselves and their territory out of Quebec if the partisans of Quebec independence take themselves and their territory out of Canada. It serves notice that, if Quebec independence does come, it will not be "roses, roses, roses all the way, with myrtle strewed in my path like mad" for Mr. Lévesque, but a long, hard road, strewn with boulders.

I do not necessarily subscribe to every particular opinion set out in this book. (I wish I were as confident as the authors that separation will not happen.) But I do most firmly endorse its general thesis, and I hope that it will be read, marked, learned and inwardly digested both by the separatists and their opponents, and especially by English-speaking people outside Quebec; most of all by English-speaking appeasers, in the province and out of it.

Si le Canada est divisible, le Québec doit être divisible aussi. (If Canada is divisible, Quebec should be divisible too.)

— Pierre-Elliott Trudeau

Attendons la réaction des *Canadiens* après la référendum et nous verrons bien de quelle façon réajuster notre démarche au besoin. (Let us wait for the reaction of the *Canadians* after the referendum and then we'll figure out the next step.)

— Jean-Pierre Charbonneau and Gilbert Paquette

What all the wise men promised has not happened, and what all the damned fools said would happen has come to pass.

— Lord Melbourne

INTRODUCTION

The purpose of this book is to put into perspective what Quebec separation from Canada is, why it will not happen, and yet why so many intelligent people are convinced that it is not only possible, but perhaps inevitable.

The book will attempt to dispel the notion that Canada is a federation of ten separate states. Canada is one state with three levels of government, each with its powers and responsibilities, but each desiring to have more control over its citizens. Canada is a single country with a complicated distribution of jurisdictions and responsibilities among its various levels of government. It has long, and sometimes unnatural, systems of communications, including transport by rail, road, air, and water, as well as postal and telephone networks. It is a common market where the unifying patterns of trade and commerce are reinforced, for better or worse, by income equalization and transfer payments between the provinces, and by a centralized banking system.

No major province can disassociate from the whole without causing great harm. Indeed, so much harm that, in practice, separation cannot occur. Moreover, there are vital areas of Canada stretching in a belt from northern Ontario to eastern New Brunswick where the two founding cultures are so intermingled territorially that they act as a hinge that locks the English and French together. The French-Canadian people, although they might vote for a ''separatist'' party and vote ''Yes'' in a referendum authorizing negotiation of greater power for the province of Quebec, would not opt for outright separation.

It is true, of course, that the idea of breakaway separation of Quebec, a major province of Canada, has become credible. This is not a commentary on the Canadian people but a measure of the weakness of character of those who have led this country over the past three decades. These political leaders, supported by some journalists and academics, have used the threat of separation to reinforce their own position. The cost has been serious polarization between our founding cultures, the weakening of the Canadian economy, and the undermining of our international reputation. We know about Quebec separatists and Western separatists, Acadian and Nova Scotian separatists, and even northern Ontario separatists. There will always be such movements seeking solutions to their problems, real or imaginary. The problem is not the existence of a separatist movement but the response to that challenge. When we give credibility to such a solution by acknowledging and encouraging it, we only magnify its importance and its harmful effects.

The myth of the possible separation of Quebec from Canada has been reinforced by two other notions: the notion of entitlement (that is the belief that Quebec could separate with its present land area intact) and the notion of the right of self-determination. These notions, in the Quebec context, have themselves taken on the proportions of myths.

In the myth of entitlement, the Quebec separatists have suggested that they would take all of Quebec with the justification that "the map is there." They suggest that the only authority over the present territory of Quebec is the Government of the Province of Quebec. Thus, if that government chooses, it could take possession of that territory. The present map of Canada, with its provincial boundaries, is a product of the division of powers within the British colonial administration since 1763 and as they have evolved through Confederation. The people and Parliament of Canada enjoy sovereignty over the land mass of Canada, and only the people, acting through Parliament, can add (as it has) to Quebec's territory, or agree (as it might) to just what part of Quebec's territory it might give up to a foreign country; for a sovereign French country would be a foreign country.

We shall also describe the myth of the right of self-determination. The authors do not take issue with the internationally-recognized Right of Self-Determination. What we challenge is the self-assumed right of separatists to choose whether or not the whole province of Quebec will remain part of Canada, as expressed through a local referendum, while at the same time denying a similar right to the minorities within Quebec. The possible realization of the myth of self-determination has been the reason why Quebec separatists are trying to create a unilingual French province. That is the purpose of the revolting sections of Bill 101 that forbid the display of signs in any language but French.

We do not believe that the separation of Quebec and the establishment of an independent French-speaking state on Canadian territory will occur. Obviously, then, it is not our purpose to write a book against separation in order that separation does *not* occur. What we do see is an encroaching poison which is gradually enfeebling the people and economy of Canada as they play out the present cat-and-mouse game of pandering to the threat of separation. This can only end in a kind of national exasperation, with a violent swing of the pendulum in the other direction: super-centralization, One Canada, one language (English), confrontation between English and French, harassment of French minorities, and so on. Essentially, and after a frightful period of wasted years, the devastation of Montreal's economy with harsh effects on the rest of Quebec, and a severe testing of the economies of several other provinces, everything would return to: Quebec is part of Canada.

Canadians, including Quebeckers, can put their time, effort and energy to more profitable use. That is one reason why we are writing this book. We do not pursue this theme because we are necessarily afraid of separation as such. Separation may be a myth, but that does not mean that it is irrational. Ultimately, while we wish to preserve the union, we are not horrified by the thought of a parting of French and English Canada. Indeed, if handled properly, there would be mutual advantages to a separation. On balance, taking economics, politics and the North American reality into account, the disadvantages outweigh the advantages for both sides.

We shall also attempt to describe the real tragedy of this period of Canadian history, which is the decline of the great city of Montreal, and the exodus of management and technical expertise that causes the decline.

This book will allow readers to judge for themselves whether or not Canadians have been seriously misled by politicians, and some journalists and academics. These misrepresentations have damaged Canada's character. But in the longer run their exposure should work to make this country stronger than it was before.

1

The Approach To Sovereignty

For several years Canada has been bemused by an argument over whether or not it should "negotiate sovereignty-association" with Quebec. Politicians such as David Crombie, M.P. and William Davis, Premier of Ontario, have been alternately praised and blamed for what they said on this subject. By and large, however, the English-Canadian public is not really interested in the question. It is as if, almost by instinct, they know that it could not be taken seriously.

Their instinct is right. The "negotiating sovereignty-association" debate has been unable to rise above frivolity because most Canadians have tried to picture the negotiations as being all about *association*. What they instinctively feel, but have rarely articulated, is that the starting point of any negotiations must be *sovereignty*. Association cannot be taken seriously unless the terms of sovereignty are established.

This has been a difficult subject for Canadians, both French and English, to come to grips with.

In impasses such as this, one tends to remember one's own poignant introduction to the "official" debate. Co-author William Shaw recalls a highly pertinent meeting on an afternoon in June, 1976. A journalist from *Maclean's* magazine of Toronto had asked him for an interview. "We met at a restaurant across from the courthouse in Montreal," says Shaw. "It was shortly after the *Union Nationale* convention held in May, 1976 at which I had been a candidate for the party leadership. I had been the first 'Englishman' to present himself as a leadership candidate for a political party in Quebec in more than half a century. My friend from *Maclean's* was curious as to why I had run, interested in my reactions to the victory of Rodrigue Biron, and what I felt were the chances of the *Union Nationale*.

"We discussed at length the obvious disenchantment that the entire province was feeling with Robert Bourassa and the governing Liberal party because of its arrogance and incompetence," Shaw continues. "There was the enormous Olympic deficit. There were the protracted labour negotiations with the public service resulting in extended closing of schools and hospitals. There was an explosion in the costs of the James Bay hydro-electric projects. There were the reductions of milk quotas to the farmers. There was a billion-dollar deficit. There was also the most unpopular, most discriminatory legislation in the modern history of the province. That was Bill 22."

It seemed likely that the voters would reject the Bourassa government. It was important at the time to develop a Federalist alternative that would have popular appeal. The *Union Nationale* had been eliminated in the Liberal sweep of 1973. But in a by-election in the constituency of Johnson, supported in part by reaction in his county to Bill 22, Maurice Bellemare, 30 years a standard-bearer of the party, temporarily put the *Union Nationale* back on the electoral map in an upset victory. Had this not happened, it is unlikely that his party would have been around for the crucial 1976 election. Indeed, Bellemare's election victory stirred the organization of the "old blues" all over the province.

"The *Maclean's* writer's interest in the *Union Nationale* political phenomenon" says Shaw "revolved around the question of how the development of a third party might help the *Parti Québécois*. It was as if the evolution of a "third force" could support his scenario of how the *Parti Québécois* would come to power and effect the separation of Quebec. A split in the Federalist forces would work to the advantage of Quebec ultra-nationalists who, in his opinion, would eventually win power and effect the break-up of Canada." That feeling, that separation could be a fairly simple matter, was and is shared by many Canadians.

The conclusion to Shaw's story:

"I said to the journalist at that time, 'I want to introduce a new word into the lexicon of Canadian politics — PARTITION. The threat of partition will prevent separation.'

"'What do you mean by "partition"?' he asked.

"'Well,' I said 'if Quebec ever attempted to secede from Canada, separation would only come into effect after negotiation with the rest of the country. Right now, the rest of Canada is prepared to make some concessions. But once there was a commitment to leave, the negotiations would have to recognize the vested interests of Canada as a nation, and Canada would have to insist on the partition of Quebec in order to protect those interests.'

" 'But' he said 'Quebec is a geopolitic. It would insist on leaving as a whole.'

" 'Quebec would not be in a position to insist,' I said, 'It does not have the means to insist on anything.' "

There is an analogy that is appropriate here, the analogy of presumption. There is the case of the young girl who begins by allowing her beau to put his hand on her knee. In doing this, the beau tends to presume that any further advances will go unchallenged.

This is the phenomenon in Canada today. Quebec nationalists have taken certain positions, notably the right of self-determination, suggesting that if the majority of Quebec citizens elect to separate from Canada and establish an independent state, that state would comprise the present area of the province of Quebec.

Let us consider for a moment the Canadian interest in the face of the separatist argument on Quebec's land area. What the precise map of a separating state would be is difficult to predict. Obviously, it would be the product of negotiation between the representatives of those wishing to separate, and the rest of Canada.

Once the emotions aroused by the proposed break had subsided, the negotiators would have to take three major headings into consideration.

The first is the part of the territory known as Rupert's Land that is now the upper two-thirds of the province of Quebec, which was not even a part of Canada at the time of Confederation in 1867, but was transferred by the British government to Canada in 1870 in order to strengthen the union of the British colonies in North America. The Rupert's Land territory would be retained by Canada without discussion. It is historically British and, by an act of the British Parliament, Canadian. It does not have any valid French historical character. Moreover, the overwhelming majority of its native inhabitants have persistently made it known that they would not be included in a separating French state.

The second heading is Canada's vested interest in the territorial integrity of the Canadian state. Canadians must retain

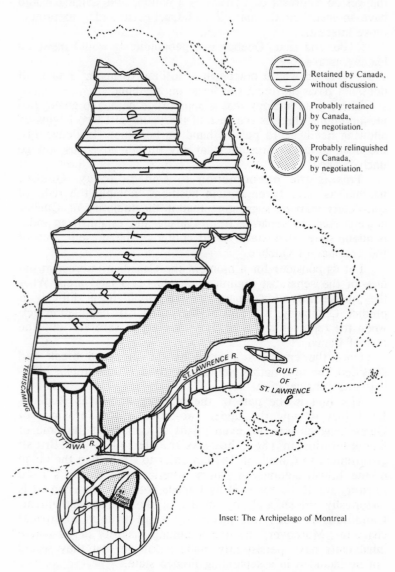

Retained by Canada, without discussion.

Probably retained by Canada, by negotiation.

Probably relinquished by Canada, by negotiation.

RUPERT'S LAND

L. TEMISCAMING

OTTAWA R.

ST LAWRENCE R.

GULF OF ST LAWRENCE

Inset: The Archipelago of Montreal

The Partition of Quebec

control, jointly with the United States where applicable, of the St Lawrence Seaway and its seaward access, and of the land corridor south of the St Lawrence River containing the principal road, rail, and telecommunications routes between Ontario and the Maritimes. No responsible negotiating team could accept a compromise of these objectives which, if conceded, would cut central Canada off from the Atlantic Ocean and split the country into two separate parts. Communication between the two parts even to air space would be entirely through a foreign country. Since the part of Quebec south of the St Lawrence River was never acknowledged as part of New France before the Conquest, and since most of that part of the province is English by early grants, and by treaties with Indian chiefs, and by the Treaty of Utrecht of 1713 signed by France, as well as by priority of settlement, the Canadian negotiators would be in a much stronger position diplomatically and juridically than the separatist negotiators.

The third heading covers the right of self-determination of a large number of Quebeckers who would opt to remain Canadian. Among the territories thus affected would be the western half of the Montreal archipelago, the Ottawa Valley including its tributary valleys, the Timiskaming region, and the lower part of the North Shore of the Gulf of St Lawrence.

The reality of the potential of partition is essential to any discussion of the separation of a territory for an independent French state.

The journalist who spoke to co-author William Shaw was not convinced. He took his qualified biases and left, no doubt asking himself whether or not he had wasted his afternoon. He was more accustomed to having his Federalist interview subjects expound on the need to convince the Quebec separatists of the advantages of being part of Canada; that the rest of Canada had to do more to make *Québécois* feel welcome in Canada; and that, above all, the rest of Canada had to do more to try to understand the aspirations of the Quebec separatists. What he failed to appreciate is that Quebec separatists are not interested in more understanding. They are not even willing to recognize the damage being done to the Montreal economy and Quebec's tax base. Everything is "normal" as far as they are concerned.

They insist that self-determination is their right, and that this right cannot be denied. Now while those who put the strongest emphasis on the right of self-determination are the separatists, thinking in terms of a people,[1] most French-Canadians do have some feeling that this concept is useful. Although they profess their commitment to Canada, they wish to retain their right to separate if they change their minds. To many French-Canadians the idea of separation is a bargaining tool.

One often hears the remark "Yes, we want to remain part of Canada, but not at any price." While French-Canadians consider all of Quebec the prize of self-determination, many regions of the province would not accept that premise. Nor, in our view, would the rest of Canada. All Canadians, Quebeckers included, have an equal say in the future of Canada.

By way of comparison, note the view of Laval LeBorgne of the Montreal French-language daily *La Presse*, who interviewed co-author Shaw during his campaign for a seat in the Quebec legislative assembly. LeBorgne spent days with Shaw reporting on the "long-shot U.N. candidate" running in a riding that had always given Liberal candidates overwhelming majorities. In spite of the warm reception Shaw seemed to have in the riding, LeBorgne was convinced that, on election day, the English would revert to their traditional voting pattern, and elect the Liberal candidate in Pointe Claire. When Shaw succeeded in achieving an upset, LeBorgne was interested in discussing with him his reactions to the *Parti Québécois* victory "We will win the referendum;" said LeBorgne "I can feel it throughout the province".

"I doubt it, Laval," Shaw said "but I'm not intimidated. If Lévesque gets a 'Yes' vote, Quebec will be partitioned." Shaw

---

[1] The authors deliberately avoid any precise use of such words as "people" or "nation" as these terms have various meanings. In the sense that the word "nation" conveys in "The Six *Nations* of the Iroquois", the French-Canadians are a nation and more. In the sense that the word conveys in "United *Nations*", the French-Canadians are not a nation. To avoid confusion we prefer to call Canada a "country". On the other hand we see nothing wrong with "*National* Capital Region" or "Canadian *National* Railways". "*National* Assembly" is wrong and misleading for the Quebec legislative assembly. We have no strong objection to "Fête *Nationale*" for the June 24 St John the Baptist holiday, although we prefer the old name.

went on to try to explain what the sequence of any negotiations would be, but, as he recalls, "I again seemed to have a reluctant listener. He had already fantasized the Republic of Quebec and any doubt about its destiny was heretical. He treated my views lightly, but he did write an article called *'Le morcellement du Québec'* (The break-up of Quebec). His article suggested that I had said that if Quebec were to separate, certain counties would opt to stay in Canada, making the map of Quebec look like a checkerboard. It was his way of patronizing my hypothesis while making it appear improbable."

Nevertheless the exposure did develop some reaction. Shaw was invited on a Radio-Canada "open line" show to explain his position. The callers were most interesting. Actually, the majority were sympathetic. Others felt that he must have incredible gall to suggest that their *patrie* was divisible. When French-Canadian nationalists suggest that they are not satisfied with the present constitutional arrangement they see no difficulty in unilaterally dissolving Confederation. Suggest that, fair is fair, Quebec's secession from Canada would result in several parts seceding from Quebec and one is thrown into the Lion's Den.

When the talk turns to separation, it immediately behooves Canadians to establish, without equivocation, that no decision of this nature could ever be made unilaterally. Unless we do that we effectively become the young lady who chose to ignore the hand on her knee, and become party to some of the irrational presumptions current in the constitutional debate.

It was in December of 1976 that co-authors William Shaw and Lionel Albert met for the first time, along with other concerned Quebeckers, to introduce the concept of partition by means of collective action. (Oddly enough both authors had lived within half a block of each other in Outremont during most of their respective childhoods, but just separated enough by age not to have met.)

An organization called "The Preparatory Committee for an Eleventh Province" was formed. Public meetings were held in Montreal and surrounding regions. The response was remarkable. There was no question that many Quebeckers, both English and French, were determined that if Quebec were to separate, central and western Montreal, the inner Eastern Townships, and the Ottawa Valley would certainly not leave

WEST QUEBEC DE L'OUEST

The motto means "Here I am, here I stay."

The Symbol of the Eleventh Province

with it. The goal was not to promote the break-up of Quebec, but to establish that one of the rationales for partition would be that if Quebec can opt out of Canada, then obviously sections of Quebec that preferred to remain part of Canada could opt out of Quebec. It was based on the example of West Virginia, which opted out of the state of Virginia because it did not wish to secede from the United States when Virginia joined the Confederacy. Most important to us was the destruction of the presumption that the prize of a positive referendum would be the total territory of Quebec.

Of course, not everyone shared the exact same motivation. Co-author Lionel Albert was attracted to the eleventh province idea mainly as a way to get English Quebec out from under the effects of Bill 22, the language law. In a sense the Preparatory Committee became an alliance between those concerned primarily with the threat of Quebec separation, and those concerned primarily with the threat to the free use of the English language.

It became clear with the introduction of Bill 101, which carried Bill 22 a little further, that the language issue was again becoming paramount. In time Albert gradually dropped his activities with the Preparatory Committee and devoted his main energies to the Quebec Committee for Language Regions which, essentially, calls for the establishment of protected free-choice language areas in northern and eastern Ontario, western Quebec, and northern and eastern New Brunswick — the rest of Canada to be unilingual French or English as the case may be. The two authors are in amicable disagreement over language regions, but remain in full accord that Quebec separation must be exposed for the hollow threat that it is.

The eleventh province movement demonstrated to us obvious weakness of the *Parti Québécois*. It was particularly effective when government ministers (such as Finance Minister Jacques Parizeau), speaking boldly about Quebec-after-separation, were questioned about the possibility that there might be a separation within the separation. They had to retreat. Parizeau, for example, argued that the Canadian constitution gave the provinces control of their boundaries. Now, according to the 1871 amendent to the British North America Act, "the Parliament of Canada may from time to time, with the consent of the Legislature of any Province of the said Dominion increase, diminish, or otherwise alter the limits of such Province, upon such terms and conditions as may be agreed to by the said Legislature . . ." If Quebec decided to cease being a province, then the constitution would no longer apply. Instead as in the case of Western Australia discussed later, the British Parliament, in theory, and Canada's Parliament, in practice, makes the final decision.

On another occasion M. Parizeau was asked about mortgage companies refusing to make new loans for development in Quebec. The minister stuck his thumbs in his vest and retorted that a major insurer had just granted a mortgage loan for a shopping centre in St-Bruno. Someone from the Liberal backbenches interjected, *sotto voce*, "But that's in the Eleventh Province!"

William Shaw chose to curtail his activities with the Eleventh Province committee because he felt that it was isolating him as a legislator, and to an extent, says Shaw "misrepresenting what I really felt was the right direction for Quebec to take. I feel that Quebec must continue to function as part of Canada. I was, and still am, convinced that Quebec will always remain part of Canada, and that when any referendum is held Quebeckers will reject the *péquiste* option. I don't believe negotiations for changing the map of Canada will ever occur. However, if the circumstances were to deteriorate and there were an attempt to establish a French state in North America, partition would unquestionably follow; and by the time the negotiations were completed, the rosy picture painted by Lévesque, Parizeau, Claude Morin and others would take on a far more realistic and unacceptable form. Personally, I do not consider partition to be a solution to the Quebec language problem, nor do I consider it a solution to the Canadian unity problem."

At the Commonwealth Parliamentary meetings in Quebec in September, 1977, and at the National Association of State Legislatures meeting in August, parliamentarians were not as concerned about a possible separation of Quebec as they were about the development of authoritarian socialist government policies in this province. It was there that the Speaker of the Western Australian legislature brought to co-author Shaw's attention the fact that there had been a referendum for separation in Western Australia in 1933. The referendum was won by the separatists, yet the vote was quickly forgotten, and the proposed separation never took place. The Australian precedent will be discussed in greater detail in the next chapter. Elsewhere we attempt to draw the scenario of what might happen if there were a "Yes" referendum result in Quebec. It is our purpose to allow the reader to evaluate these arguments. While it is our contention that Quebec will never separate, there is more to the Canadian unity problem than that. It is important for everyone to put the constitutional question into perspective. Canada has problems of constitutional and linguistic rights that have to be solved. However, they have to be solved through consideration and negotiation in good faith between the various levels of government. These negotiations are being impaired because one party is intimidating the others through the threat of recourse to an unreal option. Where, at one time, there was an awareness throughout Canada that there was an imbalance of input, there is growing reaction to the intimidation — practised by all the political parties of Quebec — to get a better deal "or else". All too often the reaction has a tragic result, as it galvanizes latent anti-French feelings.

2

Can There be a Unilateral Break?

We believe that the *Parti Québécois* will never put to the test of a referendum or election the willingness of the French-Canadians of Quebec to separate themselves from Canada. It is said in jest that French Quebeckers want an independent Quebec within a strong Canada. But a Quebec outside Canada? No. There may be questions, such as, at the time of writing, asking a soft "motherhood" question with a safety net — asking Quebeckers to "give the government of Quebec a mandate to negotiate a proposed agreement[1] between Quebec and Canada." And there may be other questions asking a mandate to negotiate a more clearly defined sovereignty-association, or an equal-to-equal arrangement, or a new Confederation, but there will be no separation question. And without that crucial question even a dozen referendums would mean nothing.

On the other hand, a "No" vote in the referendum will not carry much weight either. The separatist philosophy is not likely to go away in the short term. So, does a "No" vote matter? The separatists will still be there, preparing for another referendum. Others will be coming up with compromise solutions. We agree with Gilles Loiselle, the Quebec government's Agent-General in London, who told a *Globe & Mail* reporter[2] that the tension between Quebec and the rest of Canada will not go away even if the "Yes" proposition is defeated. ". . . the pressure in Quebec will remain." Thinking perhaps of the possibility of a "No" result, or a "third option" patch-up solution, Loiselle said "Canada has been sick for a long time. We may get rid of the symptoms for a while, but the disease remains." Of course, to M. Loiselle, the disease is some awful flaw in Confederation. But the flaw is not in Confederation; rather it is in the morbid belief that Quebec could somehow break away.

---

[1] See text later in this chapter.
[2] November 5, 1977

Consider the reception given to the Quebec Liberal Party's "third option" proposal[3] in the rest of Canada. Instead of being viewed as worthy of debate on its merits, it is, at best, described as a possible way to head off unilateral separation; as a kind of "last chance" to save the union. As Wagnerian background music we had the Pepin-Robarts report of the Task Force on Canadian Unity with its constant harping on "crisis". Then we had the ominous phrases of René Lévesque, speaking before a packed and attentive audience of the Canadian Club and the Empire Club in Toronto on January 24, 1980: "People are begining to realize this is the first time, now, we are being consulted on our future, after 350 years. It is a very, very significant moment in Quebec history."

Strong stuff! If the referendum had such dramatic importance, one would expect that the French-Canadian people of Quebec, Lévesque's supposed clientele, would be deeply interested. Yet a poll by the Quebec Institute of Public Opinion (I.Q.O.P.),[4] published only a few weeks before Lévesque's speech, gave a different impression. The question was:

Among the following subjects, which one at the present moment are you MOST concerned about?

	Quebeckers	
	FRENCH	ENGLISH
UNEMPLOYMENT	9.0%	11.6%
STRIKES*	22.8	7.8
RISING PRICES	26.6	15.1
THE REFERENDUM	14.0	34.6
ENERGY	17.5	12.5
OTHERS and NO OPINION	10.1	18.4

(* at the time there were several strikes in progress). Note that less than half a year away from the earth-shaking referendum, supposedly awaited for three-and-a-half centuries, it is the English of Quebec who are most interested in the referendum, not the French. These figures support our opinion that Lévesque deludes himself in thinking that his obsession is shared by the people.

---

[3] *A New Canadian Federation*, The Constitutional Committee of the Quebec Liberal Party, 1980.

[4] *Dimanche Matin*, December 30, 1979.

But let us, for the sake of argument, assume that our opinion is mistaken, and picture a vote in which the majority of the Quebec population did opt for separation. Imagine a scenario — no matter how unlikely — of a "Yes" vote on separation.

It was the Spring of a year sometime in the 80s. The "soft" or "mandate" questions of a few years earlier had only produced tiresome stalemate. The question was reasonably clear: "Do you wish the government of Quebec to assume full sovereignty over the territory of Quebec, preferably, but not necessarily, in an economic association with the rest of Canada?"

Referendum day was hectic. The turnout was heavy. The count was watched fearfully by all of Canada, but the result was there. The Quebec government received a 62 per cent majority in suport of its proposition. The country was stunned, just as it had been on November 15, 1976.

The following morning there was shocked stillness over Quebec. Everyone was puzzling out the next move. The telephones at Federal agencies were ringing. What would happen to unemployment insurance and old age pensions? The stock Civil Service answer was, "Don't worry; nothing will change."

The Premier of Quebec appeared on television to announce that he would not be taking any immediate action and that the population should not react hastily. He would discuss the next step with his ministers, but no changes could be expected for another six months.

The Prime Minister of Canada also came on television, advising the people not to be concerned, as the referendum was just a consultation of the electorate, and could not be considered binding on any parties.

Nevertheless, the population of Quebec was disquieted. Banks were flooded with clients moving their accounts out of the province before any feared legislation freezing funds could be brought forward. Supermarkets reported some buyers attempting to hoard food in the fear that some horrible catastrophe might occur. But still nothing changed.

After about a month people became curious as to what legislation would be brought down in the next session of the Quebec legislative assembly. Rumours flew about the establishment of a Quebec currency. But Quebec continued to use the Canadian dollar, paid Federal taxes, and accepted transfers from the Federal treasury.

Rumours also circulated about a proposed meeting between the Federal Prime Minister and the Quebec Premier to discuss the terms of a new negotiation. Still, no meeting took place. Rumours also circulated suggesting that Quebec would begin to take over Federal services such as the Royal Canadian Mounted Police and the Department of Transport. But no changes were made.

The Quebec Premier was increasingly uncomfortable. The Minister of Finance had been totally unsuccessful in negotiating borrowings as the international banking community, and even the Canadian banks, were reluctant to extend credit.

The native people in the James Bay region submitted a petition to the Queen to separate eastern Rupert's Land from Quebec and make it the North-East Territories of Canada. The petition was referred to the Canadian House of Commons. The government adopted a "neutral" attitude while the opposition parties reacted favourably. The Northern Affairs department was studying the legalities of such a step.

The creditors of Hydro-Québec gave notice that if Rupert's Land became Federal territory, they would insist that Hydro sell its holdings in the James Bay projects or produce an agreement that would guarantee ownership for the duration of the loans.

Federalists in the Eastern Townships, central and western Montreal, the Ottawa Valley, northwestern Quebec, the Gulf North Shore and the Gaspé, after studying the detailed referendum results by region, petitioned the Federal government to hold a referendum that would enable them to vote on separation from Quebec in order to remain in Canada. There was talk of withholding provincial taxes.

The Premiers of the four Atlantic provinces met in Charlottetown and approved a petition to the Queen demanding that the creation of an all-Canadian land corridor through southern Quebec, connecting Ontario to New Brunswick, be declared an absolute essential in any settlement with the Quebec separatists. Each of the four Atlantic provincial legislatures voted unanimous endorsement of the petition.

The vote in the New Brunswick legislature was particularly significant as it was a clear demonstration by the Acadian representatives that French-speaking Canadians outside of Quebec were opposed to Quebec separation. Not without some internal debate,

and the resignation of some young officials with close links to the
Parti Québécois, *the organizations representing French-Canadians*
outside Quebec unanimously affirmed their opposition to Quebec
separation.

Quebec's civil servants began to wonder whether the banks
would continue to cash their pay cheques if the crisis held. Sup-
pliers were beginning to demand Cash On Delivery for supplies to
government agencies, schools, and hospitals. Physicians, dentists,
and optometrists began to opt out of the government health plans
as rumours of the provincial government's insolvency grew.

Still the Quebec Premier made no announcement.

Everyone waited for the inaugural speech at the opening of the
National Assembly. When the Premier of Quebec walked in with
the Lieutenant-Governor there was absolute quiet in the House.
Nothing had leaked. The journalists locked up in the Press Room
with their advance copies had not managed to get anything out.

The Premier's opening remarks were about the mandate for a
sovereign Quebec. He reviewed the recent history of Federal-
provincial conferences. There were no suggestions as to what
would change; no allusions to any planned communication with the
Federal government. There was some rhetoric about social justice
and concern for minorities. That was all.

The journalists were stunned.

The following day, one by one, the newspapers of Quebec
began to attack the Premier's dream, and to write of how he had
lost the confidence of the people. Soon, tired and drawn, he would
go to the Lieutenant-Governor to dissolve the Assembly and call
the next provincial election.

No doubt there are those who would suggest that this
scenario is unrealistic. Yet, if one examines the reality of the
situation, what could the Quebec Premier do? Could he
unilaterally declare Quebec a sovereign state? Does he have
the power to do so?

Western Australia knows. When, in 1933, a majority of its
electors voted in favour of separating their state from Australia,
the British government rejected the proposal on the grounds
that all Australians, through their Commonwealth government,
had to be consulted before such a petition could be considered.

It is interesting that the Western Australian referendum for
separation had many similarities to the proposed Quebec

referendum. Yet there is little recognition of that event. We hear frequent reference to the British referendum concerning the Common Market, or Newfoundland's referendums about joining Canada, but practically nothing about the Western Australian experience even though the latter case is much more pertinent to the Quebec situation than the others. The reason may be that, even with the strong "Yes" vote (66 per cent), separation proved to be an impossibility; which compromises the credibility of a separatist option in Quebec.

Western Australia's application for separation was referred to a joint committee of the British House of Lords and House of Commons. Their report, dated 1935, makes interesting reading:

> "The essence, then, of the proposed bill is that the Parliament of the United Kingdom should, by its enactment, enable the secession of the State of Western Australia from the Australian Commonwealth. So to enact is within the legal competence of the Parliament of the United Kingdom, and of that Parliament alone.

> "It is, however, a well-established convention of the constitutional practice that the Parliament of the United Kingdom should not interfere in the affairs of a Dominion or self-governing State or Colony save at the request of the Government or Parliament of such Dominion or Colony.

> "That is to say, in effect, that interference should take place at the request of such Dominion, State, or Colony speaking with the voice which represents it as a whole and not merely at the request of a minority."

This ruling would undoubtedly apply to any petition that might be presented by a Quebec government to the British Parliament, be it direct or by way of a co-operative government in Ottawa. A "co-operative" government in Ottawa would be most unlikely. A Quebec petition for separation would have to be agreed to by the Canadian people as a whole, expressed through their Canadian Parliament, with substantial backing from the other provinces. The Quebec separatists cannot get this essential support.

Of course, there are suggestions that Quebec need not bother obtaining the permission of Canada — that it could act unilaterally. The question is — how? Without the means, Quebec has no hope of effecting a unilateral break. Rhodesia had the means; it had its own currency, and its own military; and its self-contained territory was situated thousands of miles away from Great Britain. Quebec has none of these characteristics relative to Canada, nor can it acquire them.

Quebec, rather, is totally involved in the Canadian geopolitic because of the division of jurisdictions and responsibilities within the country. The province is served as much by Federal services as by provincial services. The economic links between Quebec and the rest of the country are wide-ranging and intimate.

There is the Federal money and banking system which, through the Bank of Canada, controls the Canadian currency. Any attempt to breach this system without the co-operation of the Federal government and the other provinces would be futile. It is completely unrealistic to imagine a Quebecker receiving Federal transfer payments (such as unemployment insurance or old age pensions) agreeing that the Quebec government could unilaterally terminate these arrangements with the promise to replace them with Quebec dollars.

The Quebec government could not prevent the collection of Federal taxes. Without a legally clear constitutional mandate from the Parliament of Canada any action to inhibit the collection of these taxes would be illegal. The courts would back taxpayers who would not wish to lay themselves open to Federal charges of tax evasion.

There are other Federal services such as the Customs and Excise, Manpower, the Armed Forces, Department of Transport, Canada Mortgage and Housing and a host of others that would carry on since their functions are vital to the everyday administration of the country.

There are communications services such as telephone, telegraph, Post Office, radio and television, which we take for granted, but which are nonetheless the clear responsibility of the Federal government. It is impossible to imagine that these services could be discontinued without negotiation and replaced by new ones simply at the request of the Quebec government.

There is also transport. Although roads are a provincial responsibility, the railways and the airlines are creatures of the Federal government. Air Canada and the Canadian National

Railways are Federal Crown Corporations. The harbours are Federal property. The St Lawrence Seaway is a Federal government service. Further, Seaway jurisdiction is shared with the United States and it is hard to imagine an American government entering into arrangements with an illegal régime.

No government or political group believes that a unilateral break is possible. With all its "blueprints", the *Parti Québécois* has no detailed plan for such an eventuality because it knows that a unilateral break is useful only as a threat.

A "Yes" to a "hard" referendum question would mean that various sections of the province would begin to exert pressure for geopolitical change. The *Parti Québécois* has been working hard to make friends with the native people of northern Quebec, but the hostility and suspicion have not abated. The underlying feeling that they have been placed at a disadvantage compared to their cousins in the North-West Territories is strong, in spite of the benefits that they have received under the James Bay agreement. If there were a "Yes" referendum result, the native people would certainly reassert their demands for their land to become the North-East Territories[5]. Obviously, their relations with the Quebec government would be severely strained.

A "Yes" result would also act to mobilize opinion in western Quebec, including the Eastern Townships, the Ottawa Valley, central and western Montreal, and in other areas, in favour of a different status for their territory vis-à-vis Quebec. It would revitalize the "Eleventh Province" movement.

The most important reason why a clear, positive referendum would not take place is that, in spite of all the potential of an emotional "Yes" vote, the Quebec electorate will not give the P.Q. a mandate for separation. French Quebeckers are intensely proud of their linguistic and cultural identity. But they are also a society enjoying great material advantages. They are a society concerned about the "adventure" of separation and the socialistic, and even communistic, direction that such as adventure could take, which would imperil their standard of living.

---

[5] Two individual territories, one Cree Indian and one Inuit (Eskimo).

The first referendum question was:

The government of Quebec has made public its proposal to negotiate a new agreement with the rest of Canada, based on the equality of nations; this agreement would enable Quebec to acquire the exclusive power to make its laws, levy its taxes and establish relations abroad — in other words, sovereignty — and at the same time, to maintain with Canada an economic association including a common currency;

No change in political status resulting from these negotiations will be effected without approval by the people through another referendum;

On these terms, do you give the government of Quebec a mandate to negotiate the proposed agreement between Quebec and Canada?

YES or NO

To such a question, many of Quebec's voters answer "Yes". Many view the question as being the equivalent of "Do you wish to have your cake and eat it too?" Such a question makes a "No" answer very difficult, even for those of a sceptical turn of mind.

The principal effect of a "Yes" result would be to accelerate the exodus from Quebec of business and of Federalist-minded people. Any "negotiation" of sovereignty-association would almost immediately reach an impasse, for the simple reason that English Canada with 18 million people, not would not, but *could not* agree to share the economic base on an equal basis with five million French Quebeckers, that is, as "50-50" partners. Now, the present Canadian Confederation does a highly acceptable job of accommodating the aspirations of French-Canadians as a minority. But as soon as "negotiation" of sovereignty-association moves even one iota away from "50-50", say to "51-49", it would immediately degenerate into a tedious continuation of the dreary series of Federal-provincial conferences that seem be a feature of Canadian political life in recent decades. In that respect, little would change.

Of course, other scenarios are conceivable. For example, many believe that with a continued and accelerated exodus of non-French and Federalist French from Quebec, together with larger numbers of those now of school age becoming old enough to vote, a "Yes" referendum result is inevitable.

We do not agree with such a scenario. While the youth of Quebec have a recent record of separatism, French Quebeckers in their 20s, 30s, and 40s, have a record of ex-separatism, as noted in a convincing analysis by McGill sociologist Richard Hamilton.[6] Moreover, a massive exodus, and the consequent weakening of the province's economy, would not be accepted passively by French Quebeckers. There would then be a backlash against the separatists and the extremist authors of Quebec's language laws.

We do not predict or guess when or if this backlash could occur but, from the present situation, it is inevitable. There are some early signs, including increased attendance at English-

---

[6] *The Montreal Star*, June 8, 1977. Professor Hamilton pointed out that the belief in "inevitability", based on the political opinions of younger generations, is often mistaken. In Sweden, "in 1960, some 60 per cent of the young voters supported the Social Democrats as compared to only 32 per cent among the voters of 71 to 80 years. . . But in 1970, the Social Democrat proportion among the young voters was only 49 per cent, while among the oldest category it was now 46 per cent. . . There were defections. 60 per cent of those in their twenties in 1960, as noted, supported the Social Democrats. Studies done a decade later found only about *half of them*, now in their thirties, were supporting that party." Similar disappointments have befallen the Social Democrats in Germany and the Communists in Italy. — Professor Hamilton then described studies made in Quebec which give positive confirmation to the clear implication of the published surveys that the growth of separatist sentiment has been much slower than would be expected on the basis of the attitudes of the younger generations. "A study of French-Canadians outside of the Montreal area done in 1972 found 15 per cent favouring separation. A second question asked the remaining respondents about their position in the past. This revealed that another five per cent of the sample had at one time been favourable to the independence option. Four out of five of those respondents were now opposed to separation while the fifth was 'not sure'. . . The study found the highest percentage of ex-separatists within the 35-39 age category. Another study, this done after the 1973 provincial election, found 17 per cent of all adult Quebec citizens (including here the Anglophone population) to be in favour of separation with another six per cent reporting they had once been in favour of the option. Three-quarters of the 'defectors' in this study were between 25 and 39 years of age. Both studies, it will be noted, showed approximately one quarter of those ever in favour of separation to have shifted away from that position." The rates of defection vary over periods of time. — In other words, people change as they grow older.

language classes for adults and increased French readership of the English-language press.

Another scenario has it that once the "sovereignty-association" option has demonstrably failed, René Lévesque will reveal a harder, "unilateral", line, or the extremists like Camille Laurin and Pierre Bourgault would take over the *Parti Québécois*. Using F.L.Q.-style violence,[7] they would take control of the province and then declare independence unilaterally, with or without a referendum. A variation of this scenario has the mass of French Quebeckers, especially in Montreal, so discouraged by the decline in the economy that they opt for the extreme solution in sheer desperation.

In our opinion, these scenarios are also unrealistic. They are borrowed from such countries as Iran or Lebanon where standards of living are low. The standard of living in Quebec is very high. The mass of French-Canadians will always strive to maintain and improve that standard and will shy away from any action that they believe would undermine it.

Equally important, an armed insurrection would precipitate a military response, and the separatists know that they could never win in such a conflict.

Thus there can be no unilateral break; sovereignty would have to be negotiated.

---

[7] Expressions of support for violence are common among a certain stratum of *Péquistes*. For example, Mme Lyse Daniels-Cesaratto of Aylmer, ardent separatist and P.Q. member said, "Personally I feel sympathy for the imprisoned F.L.Q. members because they did something that was very necessary for Quebec. And I can tell you something else: if November 15 had not taken place there would have been another F.L.Q. Personally, I even thought of resorting to violence. I felt this election was our last chance. I thought, 'If the P.Q. doesn't come in, we will have to use violence to make things happen in Quebec.'" *Weekend* magazine, February 18, 1978.

3

How Separation Came To Be Taken Seriously

Many Canadians, along with observers from other countries, feel that separation is not only possible, but perhaps inevitable. Several factors led to the acceptance of this potential. The progressive reinforcement of an essential misconception through innuendo and indirect affirmation was repeated often enough so that it achieved the status of fact. It is like repeating a lie so often, with just enough determination, that it becomes accepted as truth. It can also be likened to a house of cards being continually built up until it is so high that everyone, impressed by its size, forgets that it is really after all nothing but pieces of pasteboard.

When, in the 1950s, Marcel Chaput spoke of separation, English-speaking Canada and much of French Canada took him for a frustrated malcontent, and disregarded his ideas. However, for many French-Canadians in Quebec, Chaput struck a spark. Separation seemed an attractive alternative. While the discussions were hypothetical and idealistic at the beginning, the impediments were progressively rationalized away. The hypothesis became increasingly plausible. Although the suggested means around those impediments were often irrational in themselves, they at least appeared to deal with the obstacles. To most of the separatists this was enough to give a reassuring sense of plausibility. Plausibility progressed to probability, and a movement that had originated as an emotional attachment to an unattainable dream turned that dream into a seemingly realizable goal requiring only commitment from its adherents.

An almost classic example of sublime indifference to reality is the reply to the basic objection to the separation of Quebec that was raised by André Laurendeau, the great journalist, who wrote:

"How, nevertheless, can this ideal State be created? First of all it would mean splitting Canada into three pieces: the

West and part of the centre, the East, and French Canada. In this hypothesis the English Maritimes become a small isolated territory, incapable of supporting itself. The Canada of the West and the centre lack an outlet to the Atlantic. The whole of the Canadian people would never freely consent to such a breakup. Its a chimera; an absurdity."[1]

In a typical response, Raymond Barbeau, one of the wise men of separatism, said that Laurendeau was wrong because he "ascribed intentions to the Laurentians[2] that they have never had." Why, said Barbeau, the separate Laurentia would be the most friendly state and would entertain the most normal relations with Canada, with transit privileges.

Then, almost immediately spoiling the image of the two "friendly" countries, Barbeau said that in any case, the independent French country might very well include New Brunswick[3]. In other words, Canada would not object to having the Maritimes split off, because Quebec would allow free passage across it.[4]

Laurendeau never got a serious answer to his objection. The basic question has not been answered. Professor Jacques Brossard, the *péquiste* constitutional expert, suggests that Canada's split parts would still meet at the entrance to the Hudson Strait, i.e. that one could travel from Newfoundland *via* Labrador around the north coast down to Moosonee, Ontario or Churchill, Manitoba, without crossing "Quebec" territory.[5] The *Parti Québécois* reference book *L'Option*[6] reiterates the point. Both books speak of the advisability or hypothetical possibility

---

[1]   *L'Action nationale*, March, 1955, p. 574.

[2]   The separatists' favourite name for citizens of the independent French-Canadian state, before they discovered the advantages of "Québécois".

[3]   *La Laurentie*, no. 108, 1958, pp. 240-241.

[4]   In a brief to the provincial government on Bill 101, prepared by co-author Albert, it was suggested that all establishments along the Trans-Canada Highway that cater to travellers and transport employees be exempt from the bill. The request was refused. Now the poor truck driver on his way from Ontario to New Brunswick cannot "legally" order his breakfast from English signs, or indeed, encounter any signs in English. Motorists from the Maritimes have to "run the gauntlet" of Bill 101 before they reach the shelter of Ontario. So much for Barbeau's "friendly" arrangements.

[5]   *L'accession à la souveraineté* etc., p. 198.

[6]   p. 409 (Fr. ed.)

of allowing free right of passage between Ontario and the Maritime provinces, as if that would satisfy English Canada.

The uncritical acceptance of any answer to possible objections is similar to that found among Marxist-Leninists who have evolved answers to all possible criticism of their philosophy. It is of interest that those who favour government intervention for ideological reasons also lean towards the idea of Quebec separation. Notwithstanding, there are also moderates and even conservatives among the *Péquistes*, attracted through the emotions of nationalism and group pride. In the same manner that Marxist-Leninists have ready answers to criticisms of their concept, Quebec separatists have, over the years, evolved ready answers for their critics, often in amazing detail. It is frustrating to discuss these criticisms with committed separatists.[7]

Many examples are available of economic arguments against Quebec separation. One is national defence. The *Parti Québécois* simply states that if Canada spends $4 billion on national defence, and Quebec, having 27 per cent of the population of Canada, therefore contributes $1 billion of the four, they could, for that one billion, have their own Quebec defence force. An academic study written by a former officer gave this notion some support.

In this, as in so many matters, two fundamental points are completely ignored, one rather obvious, the other less obvious, but even more telling. First, Quebec may have 27 percent of Canada's population, but it does not contribute 27 per cent of the government of Canada's revenues. Quebec is a financially "have-not" province for purposes of equalization payment calculation. Second, even now, Quebec is losing its wealth-producers, both French- and English-speaking; skilled workers, professionals and entrepreneurs. Various surveys indicate that if separation were ever to occur, at least one million people[8]

---

7 "Two senior French editors concurred that 'if you do not agree with them (the Péquistes) 110% they treat you as an enemy.' " — Keith Spicer, from Paris, *The Gazette*, April 4, 1979.

8 The Positive Action Committee report "Montreal: Present and Future", June 20, 1979, showed establishments with 20 or more employees in Montreal alone losing between 152,000 and 215,000 direct jobs under various degrees of independence, which gives a total direct and indirect loss of perhaps 400,000 to 600,000 jobs, to which must be added the

would leave the new country and migrate to Canada or the United States. An independent Quebec's revenues would be smaller than its 27 per cent of Canada's present revenue.

In spite of the obvious consequences of any separation, the arguments based on 27 per cent of Canada's population are blindly accepted by their followers who refuse even to debate any challenge to their validity.

When pressed about the economic consequences of separation, the *Péquistes* suggest "association", although few of the militant members of the *Parti Québécois* really take that option seriously. They use "association" as a tool to market independence. "Association", combined with sovereignty, would give Quebec all the economic advantages of being part of Canada while retaining complete freedom of action. The argument is that the rest of Canada needs Quebec as much as Quebec needs Canada.

A typical example is the claim that Ontario needs the Quebec market. Cars are usually mentioned first. Even in the absence of hard statistics on the the automobile market in Quebec, we can assert that English-speaking car dealers in Montreal are important. One of them is the biggest car dealer in Canada; serving a large English-speaking market. It is difficult to see the strong attraction of the Quebec automobile market if it should lose this vital section of its customer base.

One of the more striking claims concerns railways; one of René Lévesque's pet arguments. If Quebec were independent, it is said, it would ensure that she had per-capita railway mileage more or less equal to that of Ontario. The argument is that Confederation favoured Ontario with respect to railways. Now it is natural that Ontario has more railway mileage than Quebec in terms of transcontinental trunk lines. Ontario is much bigger in an east-west sense than Quebec. Ontario is also more densely industrialized than Quebec. More "local initiative" railways were built there than in Quebec. Finally, water transport has played a greater role in Quebec for more years than in Ontario. None of this has anything to do with Con-

---

dependents, plus a portion of the 225,000 jobs in establishments of under 20 employees and *their* indirect effect and *their* dependents. The figure of a total loss of a million people for the whole province would appear to be conservative.

federation. Had Quebec always been a separate country she might well have had fewer railway lines. It is highly doubtful, for example, if the National Transcontinental line would have been built across northern Quebec (incidentally opening up for development Val d'Or, Rouyn-Noranda and many other towns), if it had not been for Laurier's nation-building ("the 20th century belongs to Canada") ambition.

The argument reaches another plateau when it is considered that both major railway companies have their head offices in Montreal. Like any head office situation, it means investment favouring the "home" region. The historical connotations are of interest. Toronto has one main passenger station, Montreal has two. Sir Edward Beatty, President of the Canadian Pacific, could not bear the thought of sharing his "own" passenger terminal. For his part, Sir Henry Thornton of the Canadian National didn't want C.N. 'to use a station associated in the public mind with the headquarters of the C.P.R.'[9] Toronto-to-Hamilton, the busiest transport stretch in Canada, is served by one line, shared by three railway companies; Montreal-to-Vaudreuil has two separate double-track lines, mainly owing to head-office pride. Montreal and Quebec City are connected by no fewer than three direct lines. Toronto and Ottawa, the two largest cities in Ontario, have no direct connection. The main railway shops, where experimental and prototype work takes place, are in Montreal, in order to be near the head-office departments concerned.

An example of the lack of realism among *Péquistes* is their general attitude to Montreal. Ever since it was founded in 1642, this city has prospered because of its trade and commerce with the interior of North America. Until the British Conquest in 1760, that trade and commerce took place in French. Since then, all of the contacts with the interior have been in English. The businesses and industries that form the backbone of the Montreal economy are intimately tied to the Canadian economy. That is why English is the dominant language of business in Montreal and why 65 per cent of Montreal's businesses of all sizes are owned and managed by people for whom English is their main public language.

---

[9] *Beatty of the C.P.R.*, p. 74.

The existence of these head offices and related enterprises in Montreal is a great boon to French-speaking Quebeckers. It gives them preferred access to head-office jobs quite out of proportion to their share of the markets of these enterprises. It may well be called "the Vatican effect", or the reason why Italians occupy some 30 per cent of the top positions in the "head office" of the Roman Catholic Church, even though they constitute some eight per cent of the world's Roman Catholics.

The phenomenon has not escaped some *Péquistes. L'Option* mentions the importance of the transport and communications head offices and their central maintenance installations in Montreal. Yet the *Parti Québécois* supported Bill 22, which hobbled Montreal's English-language business. When they took power, they enacted Bill 101, which, in some respects, is even more rigid than Bill 22 as far as business is concerned. It is as if the *Péquistes* reason that since Italy is 99 per cent Italian, the Vatican should be 99 per cent Italian too.

Almost comical was the reaction of the former P.Q. Minister of Industry, Rodrigue Tremblay, when confronted by the evidence of the loss of head office employment and the evident danger of much greater losses in the event of sovereignty-association. He replied[10] that an independent Quebec would more than make up these losses by turning Montreal into a truly international business centre like . . . Brussels! Now while the rest of Belgium is covered by a kind of twin Bill 101, Brussels is a special bilingual region, where business, free to use either of Belgium's languages, or foreign languages such as English, is conducted more in French than in Dutch even though Brussels is situated in a historically Dutch-speaking province. That freedom of choice is the reason why virtually all the head offices and technical firms in Belgium have crowded into Brussels, turning it into one of the world's fastest-growing business centres. But Bill 101 is turning Montreal into the exact opposite of Brussels.

Yet such attitudes, flying in the face of easily-established facts, are faithfully duplicated among tens of thousands of ardent separatists. This sort of "dream-world" logic is used for

---

[10]   English C.B.C. FM broadcast January 14, 1979. M. Tremblay has since resigned from the cabinet and from the *Parti Québécois.*

everything from rationalizing language policy and justifying the people exodus from Quebec to explaining growing deficits and unemployment.

On this subject, the 1979 party book *L'Option*, is more judicious than previous *péquiste* material. On the other hand, it presents an organization chart of the Canada-Quebec "Association" which, in the final analysis, is as unrealistic as Barbeau's answer to Laurendeau's objection. At the apex of power of the new Canada is a council of eight ministers, four from Canada and four from Quebec. This supreme council controls the Supreme Court, the customs services, the central bank that would issue the common currency, "Air Canada-Quebec", the Canadian National Railways and the Post Office, among others. It is inconceivable that English Canada could agree that a province of perhaps five million population would receive 50 per cent control as an equal partner with nine provinces containing 18 million people. Yet there it is. To cap this nonsense, René Lévesque has begun to allow as how there could be some areas of the association in which Quebec would be the junior partner *within the "equal-to-equal" framework*; yet his followers are so obsessed that they cannot even see the contradiction.

Of immense help to the separatist movement over the past 15 years has been a systematic indoctrination of school children by militantly separatist school teachers. Many are also Marxists. Added to the ostensible promotion of the French language and culture has been teaching heavily laced with misrepresentation of history. It is suggested that the French-Canadian people have been deliberately abused by the "English" and that the comparative lack of French-Canadian economic performance has been due to deliberate suppression by the English. The innuendo is that English-speaking capitalists in Montreal have systematically contrived to block French-Canadians from commerce and technology in order to keep them in line as the "white niggers of North America". One even hears suggestions that English merchants bribed the Roman Catholic clergy to assist them in this systematic repression.

The propagandizing of young French-Canadians is one of the most reprehensible examples of abuse of the process of education in Canadian history. Many French-Canadian parents were aware of what was happening, but, when they complained, they were turned upon their by own children as *vendus*

Chart of Joint Institutions of Quebec-Canada

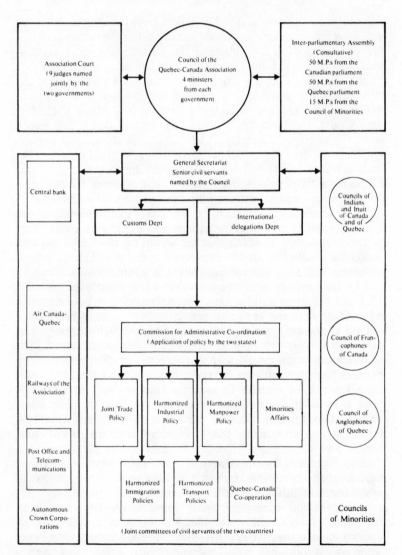

Association Court
(9 judges named
jointly by the
two governments)

Council of the
Quebec-Canada Association
4 ministers
from each
government

Inter-parliamentary Assembly
(Consultative)
50 M.P.s from the
Canadian parliament
50 M.P.s from the
Quebec parliament
15 M.P.s from the
Council of Minorities

Central bank

General Secretariat
Senior civil servants
named by the Council

Councils of
Indians
and Inuit
of Canada
and of
Quebec

Customs Dept

International
delegations Dept

Air Canada-
Quebec

Railways of the
Association

Commission for Administrative Co-ordination
(Application of policy by the two states)

Council of Fran-
cophones
of Canada

Joint Trade
Policy

Harmonized
Industrial
Policy

Harmonized
Manpower
Policy

Minorities
Affairs

Council of
Anglophones
of Quebec

Post Office and
Telecom-
munications

Harmonized
Immigration
Policies

Harmonized
Transport
Policies

Quebec-Canada
Co-operation

Autonomous
Crown Corpo-
rations

(Joint committees of civil servants of the two countries)

Councils
of Minorities

or *assimilés*, "sell-outs" of their own people.

There are no easier products to sell to young people than nationalism and idealism and self-pride. Sadly, this positive motivation was tied to the negativism of anti-English rhetoric, really anti-anything-not-French-Canadian. *C'est la faute des Anglais. Il faut mettre les Anglais à leur place* (It's the fault of the English. The English must be put in their place) were accepted slogans. These attitudes permeated the consciousness of the people. One result has been a systematic displacement of English-speaking people from the provincial Civil Service, as well as the basics of Bills 22 and 101. The language laws are in large part a response to this 15 years of the propagandizing of children by strongly nationalist teachers.

It is really remarkable that the same school teachers who preach anti-English ideas and supposedly uphold French culture and pride would not think of telling their pupils about successful French-Canadian businessmen worthy of emulation. Many of the teachers are also Marxists, belonging to one of the most militant unions in Quebec, the *Centrale de l'Enseignment du Quebec* (C.E.Q.) Nevertheless there are numerous success stories. The Perron family of La Sarre, in the remote Abitibi region, built their woodworking business from a turnover of $250,000 in 1950 to $100 million in 1979, with branches in other provinces. Among others that could be mentioned are Pierre Péladeau, head of the *Québecor* publishing group; Paul Desmarais, head of Power Corporation and perhaps the most successful "up-from-the-bootstraps" businessman in Canada; the Bombardier family of Valcourt, famous for snowmobiles but now into many branches of engineering; the Simards of Sorel, whose wealth derives from shipbuilding and metallurgy (and in-laws to former Premier Robert Bourassa who justified Bill 22 by complaining that the English-speaking had too many of the top jobs in Quebec — if the French-speaking were so handicapped then how could his in-laws have "made it"?); the Rolland family of St-Jérôme, building one of the best fine-paper mills in the country; and Philippe Beaubien, who recently brought "TV Guide" under Canadian ownership. The list could go on and on but those responsible for French-language education in Quebec are not interested in the accomplishments of French-Canadian businessmen.

Of course, whenever a negative propaganda system exists, it promotes radicalism. In Quebec, this radicalism reached its apex with the manifestations of the *Front de Libération du Québec* (F.L.Q. — "Quebec Liberation Front"). Nothing contributed more to the credibility of separation than did the phenomenon of the F.L.Q.

Canada has a history comparatively free of violence. One of the reasons for Confederation was the example of the holocaust of the American Civil War, which had ended only two years earlier. While most of the world has been thrust into periodic episodes of armed conflict, Canada has been spared the horror of full-scale war within its borders. Thus, in 1970, when James Cross and then Pierre Laporte were kidnapped, the reaction was dramatic. Canadians had had no need to develop the fundamental attitudes that could cope with such violent acts. When we needed to cope, the Federal government unleashed the draconian power vested in the War Measures Act.

It is — and may forever be — difficult to determine whether the imposition of the War Measures Act did or did not reduce the number of terrorist acts that might have followed the kidnappings. Certainly there was a large majority favouring the imposition of these measures. Furthermore, there has been no terrorism since. But it is also certain that the abuses endured by French-Canadian separatists during this period reinforced their resolve to continue.

Even worse is the probability that, in using a sledgehammer to swat what may only have been a fly, the Federal government increased the credibility of the separatist movement. Many non-separatist nationalists, especially in the media and the arts, some of whom had been harrassed by the authorities, became attracted to separatism as a result.

The Federal government then reversed its position on intervention in Quebec provincial affairs. On the one hand, this strengthened the separatist movement and, on the other, it undermined the Federal government's power to intervene.

During and following the October Crisis there was a strong reaction in Montreal's business community. Programmes designed to involve more French-Canadians in the management of English-speaking businesses were accelerated. The exodus of nervous companies was equally dramatic. A kind of resignation began to set in among Quebec's English-speaking community that Quebec would become progressively more and more French and less and less English. A slow evolution, begun in the early 60s, had become an accelerating revolution. Along with the attempt to increase French-speaking participation in English-speaking business, there were thousands of new opportunities for promotion in the para-public services, and in the Federal Civil Service as well.

French-Canadians began to feel the advantages gained from the threat of violence and, while they abhorred the gruesome murder of Pierre Laporte, they recognized that it produced tangible results. They began to accept that the threat of separation worked to their advantage. And while the majority continued to profess their commitment to Canadian unity, they also insisted on retaining the option of separation as a valid lever for underlining this advantage.

The concept of Quebec separation began to develop deep credibility. As long as there were advantages to be gained by supporting separatism, and this advantage had been demonstrated, the support would become stronger. Although many separatist supporters were using this threat to reinforce particular advantages, such as better jobs, a much smaller, but growing, number were feeling that this advantage would be even greater if the hypothesis were carried to its logical conclusion.

What Laurendeau had called "a chimera, an absurdity" had been transformed into a daily topic of comment. The horrifying image of a map of Canada, with a big hole where Quebec used to be, loomed in many minds.

HUDSON STRAIT

HUDSON'S BAY

RUPERT'S LAND

NEWFOUNDLAND

JAMES BAY

LA GRANDE R.

LABRADOR

ONTARIO

L. ABITIBI

L. TEMISKAMING

LAURENTIA

ST. LAWRENCE R.

GASPE

GULF OF ST LAWRENCE

OTTAWA R.

Hull

Montreal

Quebec

New Brunswick

Pr. Edward Island

NOVA SCOTIA

Ottawa R.

EASTERN TOWNSHIPS

PENOBSCOT R.

MAINE

NEW YORK

VERMONT

NEW HAMPSHIRE

Negotiation Reference Map

4

The Myth of Entitlement: Rupert's Land

The average Canadian, French or English, probably thinks of Quebec as a territory that once belonged to France but which, as a result of the Conquest, now is part of Canada, a member of the British Commonwealth of Nations. That is a convenient way of viewing things both for French-Canadian ultra-nationalists and for appeasement-minded Anglo-Canadians in other provinces and in the Federal government. However, this picture of a French Quebec that was conquered by England on the Plains of Abraham in 1759 does not accord with the facts. The facts are:

1) The northern two-thirds of the territory of Quebec, which is part of what was known as Rupert's Land, was British long before the Conquest. It was not given to Canada until 1870, and then it was added to Quebec in two parts; one in 1898 and the other in 1912.

2) The part of Quebec south of the St Lawrence River was also British long before the Conquest. The French also claimed this territory, but their claim was, by their own admission, weak. The first settlers in that part of the province, outside of a narrow band along the river, were English-speaking. This English priority of settlement also applies to the Ottawa Valley, to the "northern townships" that stretch across the Laurentians to Quebec City, and to the North Shore of the Gulf of St Lawrence. At Confederation, those areas were still mainly English-speaking. This is not to gloss over the fact that the French-Canadians were the majority in the province overall. Even so, the constitution, the British North America Act, recognizes the English character of large parts of the province south of the St

Lawrence River and in the Ottawa Valley, and provides certain safeguards.

There is a wealth of historical detail to support these facts. Little of this history is taught in our schools and universities, not because of ignorance or ill-will, but simply because the question of breaking modern Canada up into an English part and a French part has never been seriously considered, nor have the rights of the English-speaking in Quebec been called into question before now.

While the average Canadian may have only a hazy idea about the status of the upper two-thirds of the .present area of Quebec before Confederation, or even before the Conquest, those who have given thought to the matter have recognized that Rupert's Land could not be taken from Canada under any circumstances. The late Donald Creighton, a leading historian of the 'conservative' school of thought, wrote an article[1] to make this point. Gordon Robertson, a very senior Federal civil servant, alluded strongly to the same outcome.[2] Spokesmen for the native peoples of the part of Rupert's Land that is now in Quebec have said the same.

What about the separatists? The *Parti Québécois* people are aware of the problem but they do not know how to resolve it. One argument, used by René Lévesque in reply to co-author Shaw in 1976, is "The territory of Quebec is there on the map and we will not be disrupted by any kind of loose hypothesis like that."[3] In many ways this is the only course for the P.Q. Their hope is that that the borders of Quebec will not erupt into a major issue.

A second "argument" or, rather, set of assumptions, is suggested by *péquiste* juridical expert Professor Jacques Brossard. For example, referring to sovereignty over Rupert's Land, he writes " . . . within the framework of negotiations over the independence of Quebec, the question could no doubt be raised — and become the object of a compromise. (Thus

---

[1] *MacLean's* magazine, June 27, 1977.

[2] Dalhousie University convocation, Halifax, May 12, 1977. As at time of writing, Mr Robertson had resigned from the Civil Service during the Clark Conservative régime but was expected to resume a very senior advisory role under the Liberals.

[3] Radio talk quoted in *The Montreal Star*, December 6, 1976.

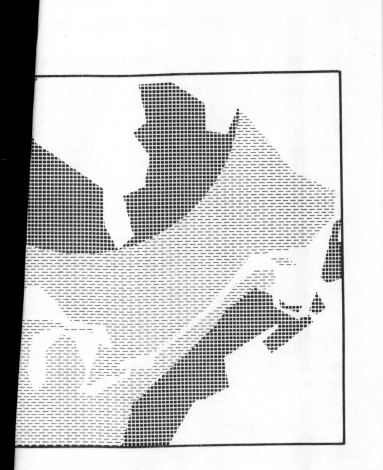

British acquisition

New France

~aty of Utrecht ending the war of 1701-1713

L'Option Map, 1713

Quebec, for example, could give up its rights to Labrador but, in exchange have its rights in New Quebec and in its share of offshore zones recognized.)'"[4] Only someone driven by his imagination to unrestrained folly would imagine that sovereignty over Labrador could be thought "negotiable" by Canada. They might as well "offer" to exchange Quebec's rights to Ontario. It would be tantamount to applying pressure on the United States for trade and other concessions by "offering" to give up New France's claims to upstate New York! As we shall see, the possible claim of an independent French state even to southern Ontario, weak as it is, is better founded, since that region was at least French territory before the Conquest, whereas Rupert's Land was British more or less all along. The comparison serves to illustrate how weak, indeed non-existent, the French claim to Rupert's Land is.

The authors of the 1979 *Parti Québécois* book *L'Option* seem to be aware of the weakness in Professor Brossard's assumptions; yet obviously believing that history could not be ignored, they resort to plain old-fashioned falsification:

" . . . it is relatively easy to show not only that the *Québécois*[5] live on a territory but also that they have been the owners of [that territory] for a very long time. The territorial space that they inhabit, and which corresponds roughly to the physical frame of the present State of Quebec, is properly theirs.

"To speak of this territory, of its boundaries, of the homeland that it constitutes, one could employ many words and explain at great length. But it is both simpler and more logical to use, for this purpose, maps. In examining closely the illustrations that follow, we shall have an exact idea of the homeland which is that of the *Québécois* and which has always been theirs."[6] There then follows a series of maps.

One picture is worth a thousand words. In this case the thought seems to be that one distorted and deliberately falsified picture is a lot less trouble than a thousand falsehoods. The first map shows eastern North America as it stood according to

---

[4] *L'Accession à la souveraineté* etc., p. 494. "New Quebec" refers to the part of Rupert's Land in the province of Quebec.

[5] P.Q. code for French-Canadians.

[6] p. 75 (Fr. ed.)

New France

British possession

1697: Treaty of Ryswick ending the war of 1689-1697

L'Option Map, 1697

the Treaty of Ryswick in 169
settlements in North Americ
1620. Even if the readers of *L*
in earlier claims arising from e
1497, Jacques Cartier's from 1
map showing the situation at a
dated about 1670 would be n
planted colonies in what is now
Why not show this? Why be so

It is not modesty that has
start Quebec's history in 1697,
began with the founding of Queb
to begin earlier than 1697, they
Rupert's Land as British. The fact
Henry Hudson first entered his b
been British, except for the perio
1713 when some of the Hudson'
trading posts were occupied interm

L'Option is not the first source
situation before 1697 even existed
cerned. History textbooks by ultra-
the map "1712", the only significa
the last full year before the Treaty
out all French hopes around Hudson
1697 and 1713 depends on the wa
"slant" his presentation: *L'Option*, tr
French "possession" as early as poss
make the English possession appear
would be the converse if English-lan
only one map of Canada prior to 171
1630 or 1631, when New France was
the English. The 1697 *L'Option* map

---

[7] The Treaty of Ryswick, 1697, " . . . stipulat
commission would be named to determine th
Kings of France and England in the region
translated from *Rapport de la commission d'étud*
du Québec (R.C.E.I.T.Q.), Vol. 3.1, p. 56, from
Privy Council in 1927. War broke out again in
apparently never began its work. During the nego
Treaty of Utrecht, 1713, the French referred to th
rather than a retrocession of territory.

shows the western littoral of Hudson's Bay, which remained in British hands throughout, as French.

The next map in *L'Option* shows the effects of the Treaty of Utrecht which confirmed Rupert's Land as British. It was the first time France officially recognized this fact. That was exactly half a century before the 1763 treaty that ceded Canada to Britain. Even on this map, the authors of *L'Option* cannot resist the urge to falsify; they show the northern boundary of New France as the southern tip of James Bay. In fact the boundary was several hundred miles further south, being the height of land. The flavour of *L'Option* is conveyed also by the fact that British territory, described in the preceding map as "British possession" is, in the 1713 and following maps, labelled "British acquisition". This falsehood is also applied to the thirteen colonies to the south.

The next map, 1763, purports to show the new British province of Quebec. It is also inaccurate, not showing the line of the 45th parallel at all and erroneously including Newfoundland, Cape Breton, Prince Edward Island and Anticosti Island all as part of the province of Quebec.

The 1774 map is fairly accurate, which is not surprising, as that was the year in which a territory called "Quebec" reached its greatest extent westward. Even at that, the map shows a strange "no man's land" in western Pennsylvania and western New York.

The 1791 map manages to ignore the existence of the new United States of America. It shows much of what are now New York, Pennsylvania, Ohio, Indiana, Illinois and Wisconsin as part of Upper Canada. Obviously history is not one of the *Parti Québécois'* strong points.

There is no map for 1809 when Labrador, Anticosti Island, and the Magdalen Islands were transferred back to Newfoundland. The 1825 map, which would show Anticosti and the Magdalens, as well as the lower North Shore of the St Lawrence, back in Canada, is also skipped.

The 1841 map is also missing. Apparently the fact that, from 1841 to Confederation in 1867, what are now Ontario and Quebec was one province has become "unhistory". This omission presumably has as its purpose support of the fanciful notion that a province of Quebec "entered" Confederation, which is impossible as there was no province of Quebec. One

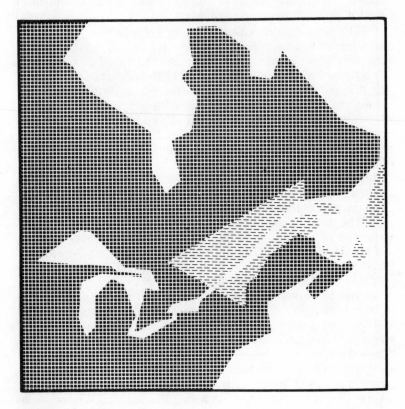

 British acquisition

Province of Quebec

1763: Treaty of Paris ending war of 1756-1760

L'Option Map, 1763

1774: The Quebec Act

1791: Act constituting Upper and Lower Canada

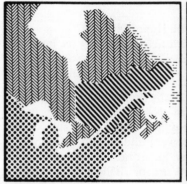

1898: Federal acts on territory annexed to Quebec

1912: Federal and Quebec acts on enlargement of boundaries

 United States

British America

*Province of Quebec

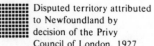 Disputed territory attributed to Newfoundland by decision of the Privy Council of London, 1927

L'Option Maps, 1774-1927

1927: Decision of the Privy Council of London on the subject of Labrador

assumes that the purpose of the notion is to assist the idea that the same province could then "leave" Confederation.

The 1867 map, that would show the original Confederation that the readers of *L'Option* are supposedly being persuaded to opt out of, is also missing. Presumably this is to spare the reader the distasteful reality that Rupert's Land was not part of Quebec at that time.

The remaining maps, 1898, 1912, and 1927, are fairly accurate.

Surely the biggest mistake made by the authors of *L'Option* was to suggest that their maps be studied *closely*!

What, in fact, is the story of Rupert's Land?

The early history of that immense territory is best summarized by the Quebec government's territorial study commission in its report on the Labrador boundary dispute:

> "It could have been thought that Labrador, now in Newfoundland, was part of New France under the French Régime. Nevertheless, the whole peninsula was not all that French. There were the territories above the height of land and other territories above the concession given to the *Seigneurs* of Belle-Isle, in the region of Hudson Strait.[8]

> "England, in fact had just as much right to the land along Hudson Strait as she had to the territory along the Bay of the same name. Hudson's Bay was discovered by the navigator who gave it his name in 1610 and the tributaries of that inland sea[9] were continually frequented by British seafarers. Besides, because of certain problems with French Governors, some of the boldest Canadian traders[10] asked for

---

[8] In other words, the original French claim to Labrador, sometimes called the "Seigniory of Belle-Isle" and sometimes, "New Brittany", never included the northern half of the coast.

[9] Including, of course, James Bay, the La Grande River and all other waters involved in the "James Bay" hydro-electric projects.

[10] Presumably the likes of Radisson and Groseilliers.

nothing better than to be free from the administrative vexations of their colony.

"Their wish was fulfilled when, on May 2, 1670, King Charles II of England granted to his cousin Prince Rupert and to others the part of North America that for over two centuries has been called Rupert's Land."[11]

In present-day terms that means all of central and northern Quebec, all of northern and western Ontario above New Liskeard, Chapleau, Lake Nipigon and the Rainy River, all of Manitoba, most of Saskatchewan, a large part of Alberta, and most of the District of Keewatin. (In practice, the Hudson's Bay Company controlled other territory as well, but this was outside of Rupert's Land.)

In the late 1680s and early 1690s the Sieur LeMoyne d'Iberville, surely one of the most impressive figures in Canadian history, almost single-handedly and several times over captured many of the Hudson's Bay Company forts and trading posts on the eastern and southern shores of Hudson's Bay. The Treaty of Ryswick acknowledged the French occupation of parts of the territory, but war broke out again in 1702. The result was a defeat for France. This was no fault of d'Iberville who ran rings round the English at every encounter. Rupert's Land was confirmed as British, this time signed and sealed "à perpetuité" as the Treaty of Utrecht stated in 1713.

The boundary between Rupert's Land and New France was the height of land between the waters flowing into Hudson's Bay and those flowing into the St Lawrence River. For a short time, between 1763 and 1774, the northern border of what was then the new British province of Quebec was even further south, being a straight line drawn from the head of the St John River, which flows into the St Lawrence from the north, opposite Anticosti Island, the line then running through Lake St John and terminating at the eastern end of Lake Nipissing. The territory between this line and Rupert's Land was part of the "Indian Territory" provided for in the Royal Proclamation of 1763.

---

[11] R.C.E.I.T.Q., vol. 3.1, pp. 54-55.

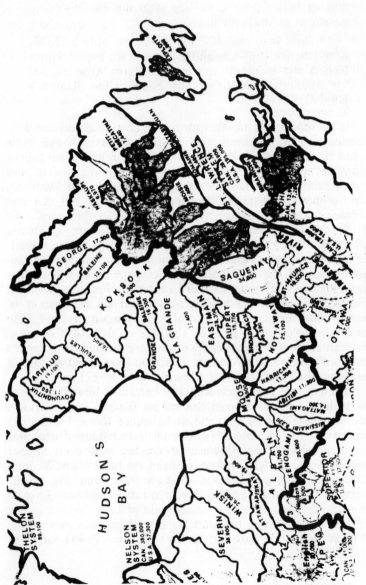

The Line of the Height of Land

The Quebec Act of 1774 restored the border to the line of the height of land. The Constitutional Act of 1791, which was the first juridical reference to a country called "Canada", reconfirmed the same northern boundary, as did the Act of Union of 1841 which created the united province of Canada. We were still not a northern country. Instead we were sandwiched between the United States of America and the Hudson's Bay Company.

One of the problems facing the elected government of Canada was the raising of revenue. In those days before income tax and retail sales taxes, an important source of government revenue was customs duties, along with excise taxes levied at the time imported goods entered the province. As always, there were those who sought ways of avoiding payment of such duties and excise taxes, in this case by bringing goods in from overseas *via* James Bay ports and then by river and lake south to Canada. In order to close this gap the Canadian government set up customs inspection along the northern border at such places as Fort Timiskaming.[12] Canada's northern border was a real border and its existence is one of the reasons why there could never be any question of giving "back" any part of the Rupert's Land territory to a separate French country.

In the 1860s, when Britain came to the conclusion that she must unite her North American possessions or see them disappear into the hands of the Americans, the decision was taken to strengthen the proposed union by giving it Rupert's Land. Accordingly, the British Parliament passed the Rupert's Land Act of 1868 by which "It shall be competent . . . for Her Majesty . . . to accept a surrender of . . . the lands, territories, rights, privileges, liberties, franchises, powers and authorities . . granted . . . to the [Hudson's Bay] Company within Rupert's Land, . . . provided, however, that such surrender [be on] the terms and conditions upon which Rupert's Land shall . . . be

---

[12] In 1858, after one incident, Alexander Galt, the Canadian Inspector-General, " . . . required the [Hudson's Bay] Company to pay the expenses of forwarding the [customs inspection] party to the Fort but promised that in future the duties could be settled at Ottawa merely by showing the invoices, rather than having the goods inspected." — *Fort Timiskaming* etc., p. 213.

The Northern Border of Canada, 1850

From a map drawn by J. Rapkin. From the Map Collection, Department of Rare Books and Special Collections, McGill University Libraries

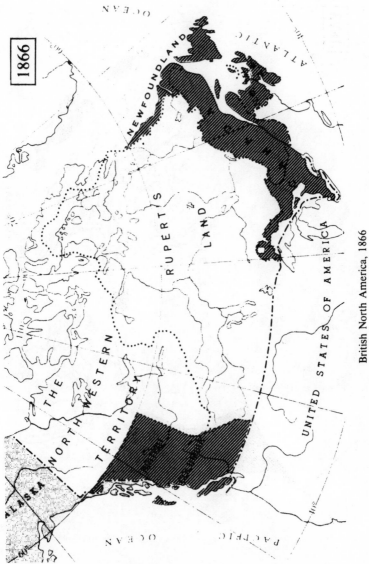

British North America, 1866

1866

ATLANTIC OCEAN

NEWFOUNDLAND

RUPERT'S LAND

THE NORTH WESTERN TERRITORY

ALASKA

UNITED STATES OF AMERICA

PACIFIC OCEAN

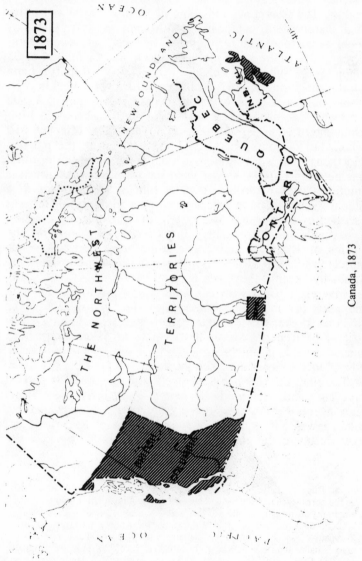

Canada, 1873

The borders of Ontario and Quebec as at Confederation in 1867

admitted into and become part of the Dominion of Canada."

The "terms and conditions" turned out to involve a lot of haggling. The Company, and some of its more vocal and influential shareholders, complained, with some asperity, that they should be compensated for their loss by being paid a considerable sum. The figure most often asked for was £1 million or $5 million. Some suggested that the Company sell Rupert's Land to the highest bidder, coyly including Russia and China in their list of potential bidders along with the obvious buyer, Uncle Sam, who had just picked up Alaska for $7.2 million. Minnesota interests urged Washington to make an offer of $10 million; but of course Rupert's Land was not on the market, even though the word "purchase" did come up in the negotiations between Canada, Britain, and the Company, and which is sometimes used by historians. The sum of £300,000 or $1.5 million which Canada eventually paid over to the Company was described by Cartier and McDougall, the Canadian negotiators, as an "indemnity" to satisfy the Company's claims on the transfer of Rupert's Land. The three-sided transaction was completed in 1870. The customs posts were closed; and Canada finally became the "true north".

Sovereignty over Rupert's Land was given to Canada as a kind of dowry in order to strengthen the "marriage" of the provinces. If ever the Canadian "marriage" were dissolved, the territory of Rupert's Land, if it had to be taken away from Canada, would, if anything, logically revert to Great Britain, and not to the departing "son-in-law".

The new Dominion busied itself with the western part of Rupert's Land, renamed the North-West Territories, from which eventually emerged our present provinces of Manitoba, Saskatchewan and Alberta. The eastern part of Rupert's Land never occupied the limelight.[13] However, the 1880s saw the

---

[13] In the Rupert's Land negotiations, all parties agreed that the eastern part of the territory had little value. In order to minimize the amount of the indemnity to be paid to the Hudson's Bay Co. the Canadian government brought up every conceivable argument to disparage the value of the Company's assets; for one, by claiming that Rupert's Land was really much smaller than was generally thought. Sec. 8 of the Cartier-McDougall letter of February 9, 1869, to Sir F. Rogers even said, "The evidence is abundant and conclusive to prove that the French traded over, and

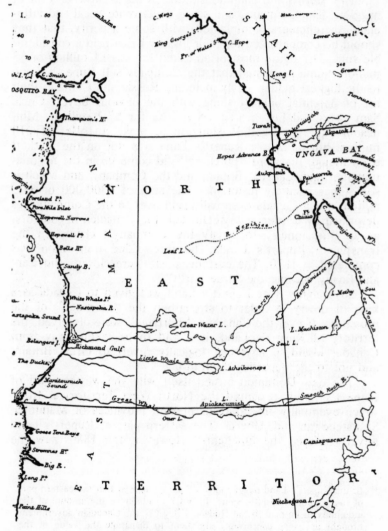

Detail showing "The North-East Territory", 1881

The Big River is now known as La Grande Rivière. From the Map Collection, Department of Rare Books and Special Collections, McGill University Libraries

first stirrings of Quebec government ambition in the person of Honoré Mercier, an outstanding politician and Premier of Quebec. Under his leadership a provincial legislative commission was established to look into the desirability of acquiring territory to the north of the province, in the part of Rupert's Land that was sometimes referred to as the North-East Territory. The commission recommended that Ottawa be asked to hand over a *tranche* of territory by which Quebec's northern border would be moved up to the East-Main River, about half-way up the shores of James Bay. Parallel moves were under way in Ontario. In 1898 the necessary Federal legislation was passed. Quebec now extended considerably farther north than New France ever had.

It is our thesis that French-Canadian nationalism is a symbol rather than a reality as a motivating force behind the Quebec government's struggle for power. It is also our belief that the French-Canadian people are onlookers, and not participants, in this struggle. The situation was essentially the same in the 1880s. At that time, many of the senior civil servants in the Quebec provincial government were English-speaking and had no interest, and probably no knowledge of, French-Canadian

---

possessed, the whole of the country known as the Winnipeg Basin, and 'Fertile Belt,' from its discovery by Europeans, down to the Treaty of Paris, and that the . . . Company neither traded, nor established posts, to the south or west of Lake Winnipeg, until many years after the cession of Canada to England. . . With respect to Rupert's Land [i.e. the eastern part, to which Cartier and McDougall tried to apply the name of the whole], or 'the lands and territories' upon the confines of the seas, bays, &c. 'that lie within the entrance of the Straits, commonly called Hudson's Straits' [quoting from the original charter of the Company] . . . a different rule, we admit, may be held to apply. . . . [but] the 'rights' they propose to sell are of little commercial value. No revenue, we feel assured, will ever be derived from them. The fur trade is the only industry the country offers . . ." Although the claim that the west was French *until 1763* was never taken up, the effect of the argument, if it were ever to be taken seriously, would be to concentrate the Rupert's Land territory in what is now Quebec and Ontario, which, if anything, detracts even further from any French character that northern Quebec could have had. — The same letter refers to an earlier stop-gap proposal by the Duke of Newcastle that all of Rupert's Land "eastward of a line passing through Lake Winnipeg and Lake of the Woods, might be ceded or annexed to Canada, in which case, nothing would be payable to the Company in respect to *that* territory."

nationalism. Like civil servants everywhere, they relished and sought out every opportunity to increase their area of responsibility. The extension of Quebec's northern boundary opened up great mineral and forest resources, and hopes of enhancing Quebec City as the best port for this vast hinterland, Hudson's Bay being ice-bound for much of the year.

At the time, the branches of the Quebec Civil Service dealing with natural resources were Anglophone strongholds. French did not become the working language of those departments until the late 1950s. So eager were the English-speaking civil servants to get their hands on Rupert's Land that they began to explore the first *tranche* even before it officially was annexed to Quebec. In 1894, Henry O'Sullivan, Inspector of Surveys for the Province of Quebec, visited the James Bay region and reported: "Nature has destined that the wealth and resources of that vast region should be tributary to Quebec, and it is our duty to leave no stone unturned to secure it."[14] Such is the kind of devotion and pride that Quebec Anglophones are ready to give their province.

In 1897, O'Sullivan again visited Rupert's Land,[15] this time exploring the country between Lake St John and James Bay, especially promoting his dream of a railway network converging on Quebec City. Other explorations had been carried on by "John Bignell on the part of the Quebec government and Messrs Richardson, Cochrane and McQuat on the part of the Geological Society." In 1912, moving even beyond Mercier's ambitions, but fully in accord with the eager desires of the English-speaking bureaucrats in Quebec City, allied with their counterparts in the Ontario Civil Service, the Dominion govern-

---

[14] Sessional Papers, Quebec Legislature, 1895. So keen was O'Sullivan that he even worked overtime at his home in Lorette, a suburb of Quebec City. The eagerness literally attains proportions that could be called "mouth-watering" as the report describes his reception at the Hudson Bay Company's Rupert House where the manager's assistant "Mr Gordon and his good wife received us most kindly. Good roasted wild geese, stock ducks, wavies, snipe and plover, with mealy potatoes, cabbage and other vegetables, washed down by a good pitcher of Bass' brown ale, go well, when one comes out of the woods."

[15] Report of Progress of Exploration in the Country between Lake St John & James Bay, for Dept of Colonization & Mines, 1898.

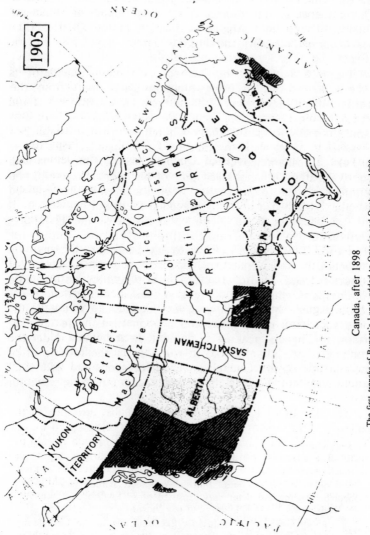

Canada, after 1898

The first *tranche* of Rupert's Land, added to Ontario and Quebec in 1898

ment passed the Quebec Boundaries Extension Act[16] which moved Quebec's northern boundary to its present location on Hudson Strait. Ontario and Manitoba were similarly extended. This immense second *tranche* of territory, asked for by no one outside of a mainly Anglophone circle in the Quebec Civil Service, now contains the famous James Bay hydro-electric projects.

From 1898 to 1960 the Quebec government, outside of its mineral and forest licensing functions, and apart from the Abitibi region, took very little interest in its Rupert's Land territory. What spark of French-Canadian interest there was came from the Roman Catholic Church, which had established missions in or adjacent to Rupert's Land, such as Ville Marie on Lake Timiskaming. (O'Sullivan's 1898 report mentions with approval Father Albanel's accounts of his overland travels, two centuries earlier, to James Bay when the French first realized that the English had not only preceded them but had also built up a thriving fur trade.) The construction of the Federally-sponsored National Transcontinental railway line from Moncton, New Brunswick to Sioux Lookout, Ontario *via* Quebec City and Senneterre, opened up a small section of Rupert's Land around Lake Abitibi.[17] Under enthusiastic church sponsorship, a few French-Canadian farmers were established there, but the life was very hard. Later, in the 1920s, some successful gold, silver and copper mines were opened, leading to English-speaking settlement. In the 1930s under the prodding of the church, and in response to the high level of unemployment, the Quebec government sponsored additional agricultural "colonies" in the Abitibi region but these were not a success.

The flavour of French-Canadian nationalist attitudes to the Rupert's Land territory is conveyed in an article written by one Pierre Letarte in which the project of a branch from the National Transcontinental line into the Chibougamau region was

---

[16] Speaking to the Bill, Prime Minister Sir Robert Borden said that the population of the added territory consisted of 8 "English", 2 "Scotch", 46 "half-breeds", 543 Eskimos, and 663 Indians.

[17] The lake drains north to Hudson's Bay but, due to the meandering courses of some rivers, some of the settlements are south of the height of land. Since that time, hydro projects have changed the direction of flow in some cases.

under consideration. Treating the project with considerable scepticism, the article stated "We have been taught that Abitibi is a region of the Province of Quebec. It is in fact mere chance that has placed it there."[18]

Even more revealing of French-Canadian attitudes to Rupert's Land is the matter of the native Inuit [Eskimos] and the Cree Indians. The Dominion government continued to exercise its responsibility for the welfare of the native people and this suited the Quebec government perfectly. A Canadian Press report of an interview with Charlie Watt, President of the Northern Quebec Inuit Association, states, "Prior to [1960] almost all contact with whites [by the Inuit] had been in English through the Anglican Church, the Federal Indian Affairs department, the Hudson's Bay Co. In the winter of 1938, game was so scarce [in Ungava] that many Inuit starved to death. The Hudson's Bay Co. handed out rations and then went to the province for reimbursement. The province refused, saying the Federal government was responsible for the Inuit because they were native people. The Quebec government argued this successfully in the Supreme Court of Canada in 1939 and, for the next 20 years, the only government the Inuit knew was the one in Ottawa."[19]

It was only after 1960 that the Quebec Civil Service, now 98 per cent French-Canadian and growing at a rapid rate, began to look for new areas of responsibility. The native peoples appeared to be an easy target. The failure of the Quebec bureaucrats to deal successfully with the native peoples is a subject in itself, but what is quite clear is that there could never be a justification for any separation that would involve Canada giving up Rupert's Land.

Some *Parti Québécois* people now say that the hydro resources of Rupert's Land would make Quebec's independence economically viable, while others, who agreed with their party's past opposition to the James Bay projects, now say

---

[18] *La Nation*, April 18, 1936. This separatist newspaper is mentioned in *L'Option*, the 1979 *Parti Québécois* book, as being part of a nationalist tradition to which the *Péquistes* are the heirs. *La Nation* was a violently racist sheet with a typical cartoon depicting Jewish, Slav and Freemason immigrants as rats scurrying into Quebec.

[19] *The Gazette*, April 7, 1977.

little. Regardless, for the mass of French-Canadian people, already sceptical about separation, the idea of not including the Rupert's Land part of Quebec would destroy whatever serious interest in independence they might harbour. No one is suggesting that the clock be turned back. All of the immense territories added to the province of Quebec after Confederation belong to the province of Quebec provided Quebec remains a province of Canada. No one is threatening to take Rupert's Land away from the province of Quebec. By the same token no Canadian government has the right to give any part of Rupert's Land away to a foreign country, and that is what a sovereign French state would be.

Rupert's Land may seem to be a kind of theoretical point now, and, indeed, should the political tide turn against separatism in a permanent way the question of Rupert's Land would remain just that — theoretical. Yet, should negotiations for the establishment of a sovereign French-Canadian state ever take place, the question of Rupert's Land would become very important and practical. The sooner the country realizes this, the better.

5

The Myth of Entitlement: South of the St Lawrence

While several authorities have pointed out the historical impossibility of ceding any part of Rupert's Land to a foreign country, nothing has been said about the legality or legitimacy of such a foreign country including in itself the part of the province of Quebec that lies south of the St Lawrence River. This area includes all of the Eastern Townships and the Gaspé peninsula.

The comparative silence arises because the status of that southern territory is not as obvious as that of Rupert's Land. And since no one in Canada has systematically examined the territorial implications of a negotiation over separation the matter has not been put forward as a subject for serious study. In a way, this has forced the separatists to make the "first move" in the preliminaries to negotiations. Again, sensing that they are on weak ground, they are trying to dispose of the subject as briefly as possible.

The *Parti Québécois* book *L'Option* does not mention the southern borders of Quebec, relying entirely on the famous maps. For his part, the separatist juridical expert Professor Jacques Brossard, apparently unaware of the danger of treading on historical "land mines", and studiously unwilling to leave any aspect of separation out of his book, devotes one sentence[1] to the subject. His contention is that the southern border of the independent French state would be the same as the southern border of the province of Quebec on the simple grounds that the Royal Proclamation of 1763 said so! No suggestion is offered by Professor Brossard, not a man normally at a loss for words (his book runs to 800 pages), to explain why his proposed border of the independent French state should be accepted by Canada simply because King George III proclaimed it.

---

[1] *L'accession* etc., p. 487.

The King of course, proclaimed that boundary only to divide his new Province of Quebec from his older provinces of New York, New Hampshire,[2] Massachusetts Bay,[3] and Nova Scotia.[4] It was made clear that the historic line between French territory and English territory was the St Lawrence River; French to the north; English to the south. The new Province of Quebec was officially defined "as comprehending all such Part of Canada on the North Side of the River St. Lawrence, and all such Parts of His Majesty's antient Colonies of Nova Scotia, New England, and New York on the South Side of the said River as lie within the Limits above mentioned . . ."[5]

In the supporting documents for the King's Commission to General Murray, the first Governor of Quebec province, the royal commissioners proposed "to your majesty, as it may be a means of hereafter removing any objection which may be taken on the part of the Province of Massachusetts Bay to the Southern Line of Quebec, as far as it concerns their Northern Limits, for if such Objection should be made, and it Should appear upon examination they have any just ground of Complaint, it will be in your Majesty's power to make them a reasonable Compensation by allowing their Jurisdiction to extend as far Eastward as the River St. Croix, between which and the River Penobscot they have lately made some considerable Settlements."[6]

Apparently there was "just ground for Complaint", for the advice was followed. King George III took conquered French territory north of the St Lawrence, added to it pieces of the older British provinces south of the St Lawrence, and compensated those older provinces by giving one of them what is now the eastern part of the state of Maine, previously part of Nova Scotia. The Royal Proclamation, finally signed on October 7, 1763, was an instrument of the Conquest and has always so

---

[2]   Including the present state of Vermont (until 1764, when Vermont was transferred to New York. It became a state in 1791.)

[3]   Including the present state of Maine.

[4]   Including the present province of New Brunswick.

[5]   Lord Halifax to the Board of Trade, September 19, 1763. "The Limits" refers to the boundaries north of the St Lawrence.

[6]   Commissioners for Governors, Lords Hillsborough, Halifax, and Sandwich, October 6, 1763.

been regarded by French-Canadian historians. Provision was made in it for large-scale British settlement in the townships, with special status and privileges for the Anglican clergy. In no way was the new province of Quebec to be a haven or reserve for the French-Canadians.

In this, as in many other matters, the separatists have not yet realized that they cannot have their cake and eat it too. The fundamental aim of separation is to overturn the British Conquest, which was formalized in the Royal Proclamation. They cannot overturn the proclamation and still claim its benefits. The question naturally arises: what would be the legitimate southern boundary of an independent French state? To answer this question we must go back in time to the situation not in 1763, but in 1755, before the Seven Years' War began. After all, the purpose of separation is to reverse the British Conquest or, in other words, to proceed as if that war had never taken place.

Hence, any future negotiations between Canada and French separatists over the part of Quebec south of the St Lawrence River must take up more or less where the negotiations between Britain and France over that territory broke off in 1755. It is, therefore of more than passing interest to know where those negotiations then stood. Fortunately, a splendid study of this subject was made in the 1930s by Max Savelle under a grant from the Carnegie Endowment for International Peace.[7] But, before the state of the negotiations in 1755 is described, it is useful to summarize the historical background, for Britain and France never did agree where, on the south of the St Lawrence River, the boundary was.

The situation prior to 1748 is nicely summarized in the report of the Quebec government territorial commissioners:

"The French Régime itself was characterized by the undefined nature of its administrative boundaries, and that vagueness was to be evident in the various aspects of the Régime: trading empire, military colony or populated colony. New France included numerous territories that were poorly delimited, whose boundaries were contested and disputed, even militarily.

---

[7] *The Diplomatic History of the Canadian Boundary 1749-1763.*

"Where did New France, Louisiana, and Acadia
end? Where did the territories of the thirteen British
colonies begin? What were truly the borders of the
French, British and even the Dutch colonial empires?
Actually, the boundaries shifted backwards and for-
wards following the ups and downs of victories and
defeats. This was as true of the St Lawrence Valley as
it was of the Great Lakes, Ohio and western regions."[8]

Both Britain and France hotly disputed possession of the
wide belt of unoccupied territory stretching between the French
seigniories strung along the shores of the St Lawrence and
Richelieu rivers on the north, and the English settlements
around Albany and in western Massachusetts and southern
New Hampshire on the south. The interest was strategic. The
history books are filled with accounts of violent events that
involved raids, massacres, forts changing hands, friendly Indians, hostile Indians and the like. Even today, much of the then
disputed territory is sparsely settled and rather heavily depen-
dent on tourist industries.

As far as the British were concerned the northernmost
claim was the 48th parallel, the northern boundary of the grant
made in 1620 to the Plymouth Council for New England. This
would have put Montreal, Quebec City and even Tadoussac in
British territory. A more important claim was that of New
Scotland (Nova Scotia), including what is now New Brunswick,
but which then extended to the shores of the St Lawrence and
included the entire Gaspé peninsula.

An important Dutch map published in 1657 shows New
Belgium (later New York) as bounded on the north by the St
Lawrence River and on the east by the Richelieu River and
Lake Champlain. It, at least, allowed that some territory below,
that is east of, the Richelieu, was "part of New France".

The French were also assertive in their map-making,
although more in the direction of the interior of the continent
than south of the St Lawrence. For example, Louis Joliet's
pretty map of 1673-74 shows a grand sweep of the words
Nouvelle France. The British colonies are named in tiny letters

⁸ R.C.E.I.T.Q., Vol. 3.1, p. 47.

close to the Atlantic coast. No lines are drawn, but the place-
ment of the flourishes on the letters indicates that Albany
might be considered French. Joliet, perhaps wisely, avoided
drawing any boundaries.

In 1713, by the Treaty of Utrecht, France acknowledged
that British sovereignty extended over all the lands of the
Iroquois. What those lands were was a matter of disagreement
between the two countries. At least one map-maker simply
ignored that particular provision. Guillaume Delisle, Geographer to King Louis XIV of France, produced a high-
quality map of Louisiana, which experts date approximately
1718, in which a line is drawn east from the crest of the
Allegheny Mountains to a point near the site of the present
Harrisburg, Pennsylvania, then due north for some distance
and then gradually northeast in such a way as to skirt the
English settlements around Albany. Such a line would seem to
have contravened the then recent Treaty of Utrecht as it would
have thrown the Iroquois heartland into New France.

An important map by John Mitchell, 1755, shows the
province of New York extending to the St Lawrence and
Richelieu rivers, but it also shows the province of New England
(more or less another name for Massachusetts), as well as
Nova Scotia, extending in such a way as to leave no French
territory south of the St Lawrence. Historians hold the Mitchell
map in high regard. A map by Thomas Jefferys, contemporary
with Mitchell's, supports the same claims. It clearly shows the
line of the Chaudière and Kennebec rivers, from the St Lawrence to the Atlantic, north to south, as the boundary between
Nova Scotia and New England. (Jefferys was Geographer to
the Prince of Wales, afterwards George III.)

A map by Ellis Huske (or his son John), also dated 1755,
is even more assertive on the subject of the northern limits of
New York, claiming that the Ottawa River, and not the St
Lawrence, was the dividing line west of Montreal, placing what
is now southern Ontario in New York. Like Mitchell and Jeff-
erys, he shows the territory east of the Richelieu as part of
Massachusetts Bay; in this case naming what is now the Eastern
Townships and the Beauce as well as the state of Maine "The
County of York". In his text, Huske argued that Britain should
press France to remove her " . . . seven Villages in the
Province of Massachusetts-Bay on the South Banks of the St

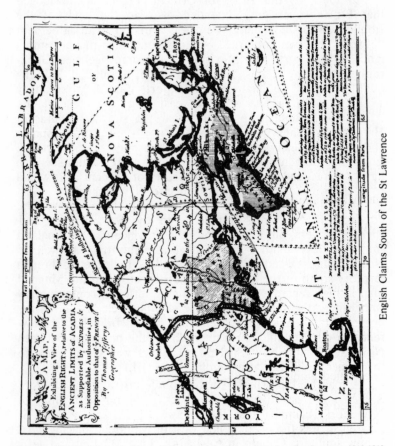

Drawn by Thomas Jefferys. End-paper in *The Diplomatic History of the Canadian Boundary, 1749-1763*

English Claims South of the St Lawrence

Lawrence River between the Isle of Orleans and the Mouth of the Iroquois or Sorrel⁹ River."

While the British and the French in the New World were sniping at each other through map-making, military forays and the construction of outposts, the diplomats were at work in the Old World, trying to arrive at a boundary that both kingdoms could recognize. A joint Anglo-French commission was authorized by the Treaty of Aix-La-Chapelle in 1748. The commission met in Paris in 1753 and sat until 1755, but could not agree. Losing patience with the commission, King Louis XV of France and King George II of England authorized direct negotiations. Heading the negotiations in the final stage of the diplomatic bargaining were Sir Thomas Robinson, for Britain, and the Duke de Mirepoix, Ambassador in London, for France.

An important feature of all these negotiations was the French concern for their position in what are now Canada's Maritime provinces, and about their sovereignty over the Ohio and Mississippi valleys. They did not press their claims south of the St Lawrence River with any vigour, perhaps less because of early English grants than because they had accepted, by the Treaty of Utrecht 40 years before, British hegemony over the lands of the Iroquois. Today, the Caughnawaga Indian Reserve, on the south bank opposite Montreal, is a living reminder that the Iroquois territory extended to the shores of the St Lawrence.

On March 22, 1755, the Duke de Mirepoix, apparently acting on secret instructions from King Louis, " . . . not only took the initiative but also went far in the direction of compromise".¹⁰ He proposed that a narrow *lisière* or buffer zone be established along the south shores of Lake Ontario and the St Lawrence River down to a point near Quebec City and then be extended straight across what is now New Brunswick to a point near the site of the present Moncton. Within the *lisière*, French establishments would be allowed, but only in the part along the St Lawrence. The purpose of the eastern extension was to permit overland winter communication between New France and the French-held Island of St-Jean (now Prince Edward

---

⁹ The Richelieu.
¹⁰ *The Diplomatic History* etc., p. 69.

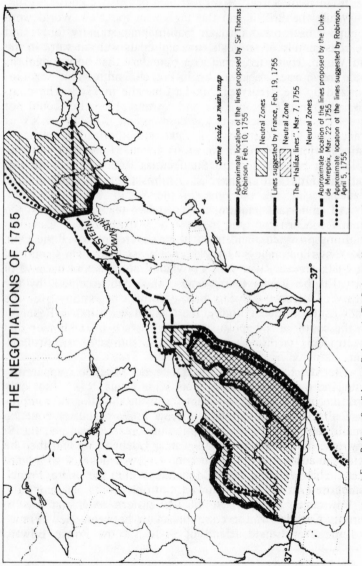

THE NEGOTIATIONS OF 1755

EASTERN TOWNSHIPS

37°

37°

Same scale as main map

Approximate location of the lines proposed by Sir Thomas Robinson, Feb. 10, 1755

Neutral Zones

Lines suggested by France, Feb. 19, 1755

Neutral Zone

The "Halifax lines", Mar. 7, 1755

Neutral Zones

Approximate location of the lines proposed by the Duke de Mirepoix, Mar. 22, 1755

Approximate location of the lines suggested by Robinson, April 5, 1755

From Professor Savelle's map. End-paper in *The Diplomatic History of the Canadian Boundary, 1749-1763*

Island). The line proposed by the French acknowledged as British the part of the present province of Quebec known as the Eastern Townships. The counter-proposal by Robinson suggested that the boundary simply be the St Lawrence itself, with a neutral zone southward. This offer, made on April 5, 1755, was the last major move before the war broke out. All subsequent negotiations took place in the light of the outcome of the war itself.

It is within the frame of the last French proposal and the last British proposal that negotiations between a generous Canada, graciously and gallantly (and those are the words) willing to leave aside the outcome of the Seven Years' War and proceed as if the Conquest had not taken place, and the representatives of a separating French state, might begin. In 1755, the British wanted one shore of the St Lawrence River and Lake Ontario so that they could navigate those waters freely. In the 1980s Canada, with much greater strategic necessity, would insist that the St Lawrence Seaway, which hugs the south shore of the St Lawrence down to Montreal and then continues as the ship channel of the river itself, remain in her hands by Canadian possession of the south shore down to the river's mouth.[11]

In 1755, the French wanted to keep the land connection to their maritime holding in what is now Prince Edward Island. Now, for the same reason, Canada would insist on keeping the south shore of the St Lawrence, in order to retain her land corridor connecting Ontario with the Maritime provinces.

The seaway and the land corridor are two points on which Canada cannot yield. With the part of Quebec south of the St Lawrence in Canadian hands, the separatists would need to cross Canadian territory in order to trade with the United States. This would be less of a handicap than that which would be imposed on Canada if she were cut in two.

We cannot predict the outcome of territorial negotiations between Canada and the separatists. Indeed, we do not believe that matters will ever reach that stage. Yet it is worth quoting

---

[11]   As it happens, most of the pilots' stations and navigation aids are on the south shore.

Professor Savelle's conclusion about the negotiations that broke off in 1755:

> "Had France then been willing to accept even the extreme British claim, Canada at worst would have been bounded, along its southern frontier, by a neutral zone, or series of zones. Such a zone would have stretched along the southern shore of the St Lawrence . . . But Canada would have remained French; and the British would have been committed not only to a recognition of French ownership but also a clearly marked boundary line which would have placed a definite limit upon British expansion westward."[12]

Perhaps it is needless to make the point, but Professor Savelle might have added that if France had accepted the farthest northern boundary in the British proposal, she would still have enjoyed hegemony over all of the North American west, north of Mexico, all the way to the Rocky Mountains. It is fair speculation to suggest that given a continuing strong French base along the St Lawrence and the Mississippi, France would not have been disposed to enter into the Louisiana sale, and that Quebec City would today be capital of a country including, among others, what are now the states of Wisconsin, Michigan, Indiana, Illinois, Missouri, Mississippi and Louisiana, then north again to Nebraska and Wyoming. In competition with the Hudson's Bay Company to the north, the thirteen British colonies to the east, and the Spaniards to the south and west, France would have had a fighting chance at control over additional huge sections of the interior of North America. Because the area now known as the Eastern Townships could not be had . . . History is more complicated than such might-have-beens, but . . . who knows?

The French future in the interior of North America would finally have depended on the capability and will to build and defend viable French communities at Detroit, St Louis, Des Moines, St Paul, Duluth and north into what is now Canada. The characteristic reluctance of the French to emigrate in large numbers probably obviates such a scenario. French officials,

---

[12] *The Diplomatic History* etc. p. 152.

even including such determined ministers as the Duke de Choiseul, attached much greater importance to fishing rights in the Gulf of St Lawrence and to various islands in the West Indies than to the North American interior.[13] So, for that matter, did most British officials. Even Pitt, the anti-French 'warmonger' held this view. The only reason why Pitt decided in favour of conquering Canada, including the Ohio and Mississippi valleys, was to satisfy the demands of the thirteen colonies. So it still comes down to the fact that as long as France would not or could not populate her colonies, she was bound to lose them.

In 1755 the French did not accept a boundary line. A few months later the Seven Years' War began. At the end France gave up her Canadian colony including the Ohio and eastern Mississippi valleys. France was out of the picture so there was no longer any need to delineate between French and British territory south of the St Lawrence. It was now all British.

To cast the boundary between the province of Quebec on the north and the provinces of New York, New Hampshire, Massachusetts Bay and Nova Scotia on the south, the Royal Proclamation of 1763 used the junction of the 45th parallel and the St Lawrence River (opposite the site of the present Cornwall, Ontario) as a starting point. Then the boundary followed the line of the 45th parallel eastward from the St Lawrence to the head of the Connecticut River,[14] then along the height of land between St Lawrence and Atlantic waters, and finally the Bay des Chaleurs. While it might appear to some that the line of the 45th parallel and the St Lawrence/Atlantic height of land looks like the reflection of some sort of compromise between former English claims and former French claims, that is not logically possible. A compromise can only take place between opposing parties. The line was drawn solely to satisfy whatever requirements the bureaucrats of Whitehall wished to take into account.[15] There was absolutely no "French" interest represented. No doubt one of the more important motives for

---

[13]   The one Frenchman who not only realized the importance of the North American interior but also, like d'Iberville in earlier days, displayed great military leadership, was the Marquis de la Galissonnière.

[14]   The west branch, Hall's Stream (defined in the treaty of 1783).

[15]   Bruce Hutchison believes that this "paper boundary" would not, of itself,

assigning the south shore of the St Lawrence to Quebec was to prevent the provinces of New York and Massachusetts Bay acquiring possession of seaward access on the St Lawrence in addition to the Atlantic ports that they already possessed. Such a line would have given those two colonies too much power compared to the others. There is evidence that the Board of Trade, which was primarily responsible for drawing the line, attached great importance to maintaining a "balance of power" among the various colonies.

The same boundary line, by and large, was confirmed by the Quebec Act of 1774. In 1783, the Treaty of Paris between Great Britain and the new United States of America reconfirmed the boundary between the province of Quebec and the states of New York, New Hampshire and Massachusetts (Maine), details of which were finally settled by Lord Ashburton, for Great Britain, and Daniel Webster, for the United States, in the 19th century.

The part of Quebec's southern border that happens to be part of Canada's international boundary was strictly a British creation to divide British colonies, and had nothing to do with delineating former French territory from that which had heretofore been British. Nor could the rest of Quebec's southern border, which is the interprovincial boundary with New Brunswick, play such a role.

As alluded to earlier, the province of Nova Scotia extended north to the St Lawrence River and included the Gaspé peninsula; and the Royal Proclamation of 1763 specifically took that part of Nova Scotia north of what is now the New Brunswick-Quebec boundary line and made it part of the new province of Quebec. So the Gaspé, too, has the strongest English claim from an entitlement point of view.

As in the case of the Eastern Townships, the Gaspé transaction was strictly a transfer of land between British provinces to suit Whitehall's convenience, and nothing to do with "giv-

---

have stood up to pressure from the thirteen colonies. "No one imagined then that the line, wherever it might lie, would be the boundary of two separate nations." — *The Struggle for the Border*, p. 128.

ing" the Gaspé to a "French" province. In fact, when the time came to divide what remained British of the huge province of Quebec created in 1774 into two provinces, Upper Canada and Lower Canada, Whitehall officials preferred to add the Gaspé to the recently-created province of New Brunswick, which had been carved out of Nova Scotia in 1784. Before incorporating this change into the Constitutional Act, then being drafted, William Grenville, Secretary of State in charge of colonial affairs, consulted Lord Dorchester who was then at Quebec (by letter dated October 20, 1789), in which he said:

> "In settling this point of the Boundaries it will also be a question, whether the Fishing Settlement in Gaspé may not with advantage be annexed to the Government of New Brunswick rather than to be left as a part of that of Lower Canada under the system now proposed to be established particularly as the local Circumstances of that District might render a representation of it in an Assembly at Quebec extremely difficult if not impracticable."

Dorchester had his doubts, and replied on February 8, 1790:

> "The District of Gaspé it seems best for the present to leave annexed to the Province of Lower Canada, on account of its commercial connections with this province, and because, notwithstanding its distance, the communication of it with Quebec by water, is easier than its access to the seat of the Government of New Brunswick, in the present condition of that province ."

So the Gaspé was "for the present" excluded from New Brunswick. Again, there could be no consideration of a "French" interest, notwithstanding that Lord Dorchester, the father of the Quebec Act, was a strong supporter of French rights. He did not persuade Britain to put the Gaspé into Lower Canada in order to make it French. At that time the region was only just opening up to settlement[16] — and the first settlers were United Empire Loyalists, followed by English colonists

---

[16] There had been a French Roman Catholic mission but no settlement.

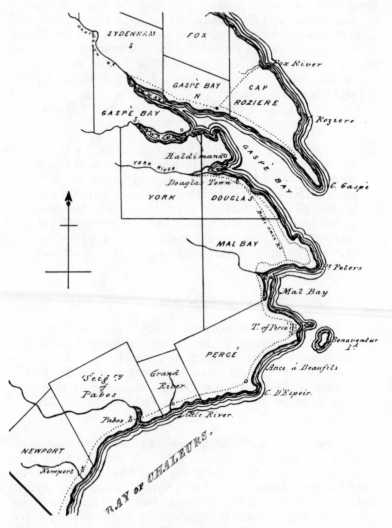

The Eastern Gaspé, 1854

From a Township Survey map, Province of Canada. From the Map Collection, Department of Rare Books and Special Collections, McGill University Libraries

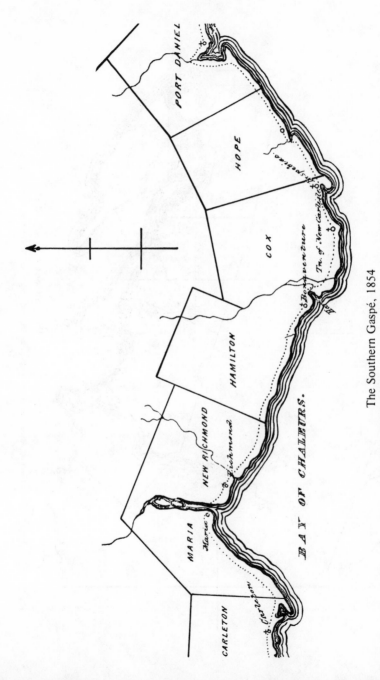

The Southern Gaspé, 1854

From a Township Survey map, Province of Canada. From the Map Collection, Department of Rare Books and Special Collections, McGill University Libraries

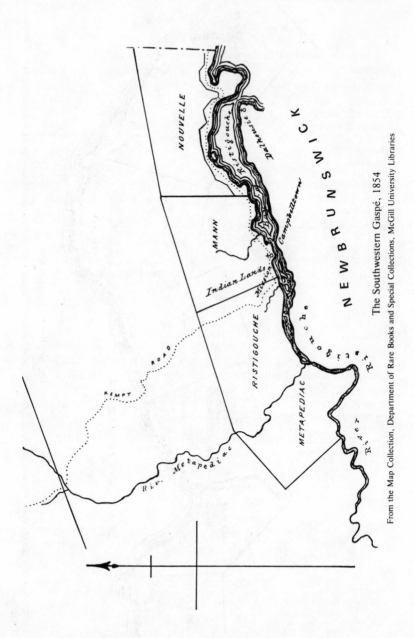

The Southwestern Gaspé, 1854

From the Map Collection, Department of Rare Books and Special Collections, McGill University Libraries

TABLE

Population by Language Group — Gaspé, 1851-52

Township:	English	French	Maritime*
Gaspé County (East Part):			
Newport	93	253	2
Pabos (Seigniory)	261	387	29
Grande-Rivière	83	594	12
Percé	865	1273	22
Malbay	396	379	5
Douglass	754	65	0
York	133	28	2
Gaspé Bay, South	421	5	17
Gaspé Bay, North	239	2	7
Sydenham	40	0	0
Cap Desrosiers	358	426	1
Fox	99	485	0
Bonaventure County (East Part):			
Port Daniel	423	368	35
Hope	558	523	26
Cox	1009	649	35
Hamilton	106	918	7
New Richmond	770	470	34
Maria	416	877	56
Carleton	47	798	10
Bonaventure County (West Part):			
Nouvelle	626	610	73
Mann	502	54	13
Ristigouche	326	71	108
Métapedia	117	2	207

*No distinction made between Maritime province natives of French, and of non-French, origin.

from the Channel Islands, and a scattering of Acadians. French-Canadian settlement in the Gaspé began much later. Even as late as the 1850s, the Gaspé was still half English-speaking. René Lévesque was born there, but his parents were born elsewhere.

While the present southern boundary of Quebec is an entirely legitimate border between Canada and the United States, and between the Canadian provinces of Quebec and New Brunswick, it has no value whatsoever as a potential southern boundary of an independent French country. As long as Quebec is a province of Canada its southern boundary is clear. But if separation were to occur then Canada could not agree to relinquish to a foreign country territory that was not originally French, that was added to the province of Quebec strictly to suit British administrative convenience and objectives,[17] that was in large part first settled by the English-speaking and which is of vital strategic importance to Canada's sea traffic with the Great Lakes and to her overland communication with her Maritime provinces.

While not denying the pleasures of historical research, we wish to make clear that we are not eager to raise questions that appear to be matters of French against English. It is particularly painful to bring such questions up in the context of the history of settlement in the Eastern Townships, for probably nowhere else in Canada do French and English live side by side in such harmony and mutual respect.

We have often been struck by René Lévesque's inability to comprehend that the emotions that his ultra-nationalist movement unleash are capable of arousing equally strong emotions

---

[17] An example of these concerns occurs in the exchange between Grenville and Dorchester mentioned above. The latter wrote, "But the Bay of Chaleurs being subject to different Governments, particularly during the present uninhabited state of that part of New Brunswick, gives an opportunity to ill disposed persons to elude the controul of the law, to the detriment of the Fisheries, and good order; a clause to remedy this Evil is therefore inclosed . . . "

among English-speaking Canadians. Restrictive language laws such as Bill 22 and Bill 101 stimulate resentment. Professor David Rittenhouse of Bishop's University at Lennoxville in the Eastern Townships spoke of the "peculiar feeling" experienced at a special "colloquium for minorities" organized by Quebec's language minister Camille Laurin at Sherbrooke (of which Lennoxville is a neighbour and suburb), at which the English language, the language of the first settlers in the area, was placed on the same footing as Greek, Italian, and other mother tongues of recent immigrants. "One was made to feel that one's six generations of forebears in the area counted for nothing; as if one were a newly-arrived immigrant in one's own country,"[18] said Rittenhouse, son of Charles Rittenhouse, and like his famous father, a specialist in the dramatic arts. The Eastern Townships is where Canada's English-language summer theatre movement began.

But the discussion of priority of settlement is not just a case of a pair of repressed Anglo-Quebeckers "letting off steam". It is a small but integral part of Canada's case in any future negotiations over sovereignty for a separate French state. If there is any doubt about it, the fact that the separatists harp on the false theme that "Quebec", meaning all of the province, has always been the home of the French-Canadians, and that other Quebeckers are only late-comers, proves our point.

The original French settlements lay along both shores of the St Lawrence from below Quebec City to just above Montreal, along the lower reaches of the Chaudière River, and along the lower portion of the valley of the Richelieu. These settlements were in seigniories or feudal domains granted by the King of France, usually square or rectangular in shape. The portions of the seigniories more than two or three miles from the river banks were rarely settled or cultivated or named by the French nor even visited by them for fear of attack by Indians. Regulations against unauthorized travel in the wild further discouraged local exploration.

The King of France also granted some scattered seigniories along the Ottawa River, along the lower St Lawrence and in the

---

[18] Talk delivered at a symposium of the West Island Citizens' Association, Pointe Claire, November 24, 1979.

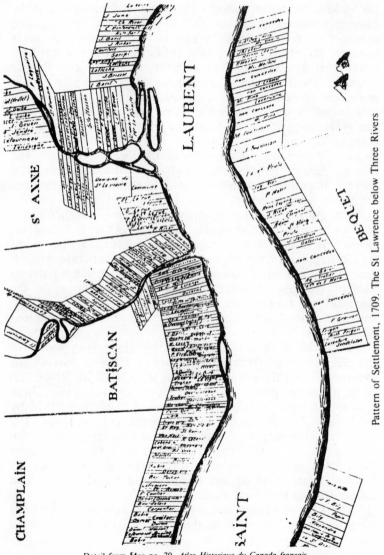

Detail from Map no. 70, *Atlas Historique du Canada français*

Pattern of Settlement, 1709. The St Lawrence below Three Rivers

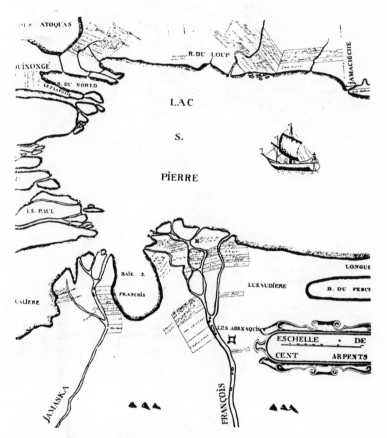

Pattern of Settlement, 1709, Confluence of the St Francis and St Lawrence rivers ("Lake St-Pierre")

Detail from Map no. 71, *Atlas Historique du Canada français*

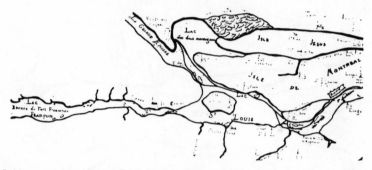

Parishes at and above Montreal. The Parish of Vaudreuil, north of Les Cèdres, is omitted, apparently in error.

Map of anonymous authorship, in the Seminary of Quebec

Parishes along the St Lawrence, same map.

Compare to the 1709 maps. In general, in 1790, there was still room in the seigniories to accommodate the increase in population.

From Map no. 80, *Atlas Historique du Canada français*

French-Canadian Parishes Towards 1790
30 Years After the Conquest

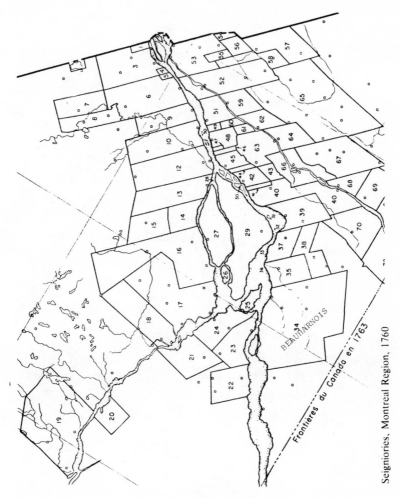

Seigniories, Montreal Region, 1760

See next map for key to numbers. Some of these seigniories existed only on paper. Note that the western boundaries of the seigniories of Rigaud (#21) and Nouvelle-Longueuil (#22) form the present boundary between Ontario and Quebec. The seigniory of Pointe-à-l'Orignal (#20) was left in Upper Canada, now Ontario. Although dated 1674, it existed only on paper, as was also the case of the other two named.

From Map no. 75, *Atlas Historique du Canada français*

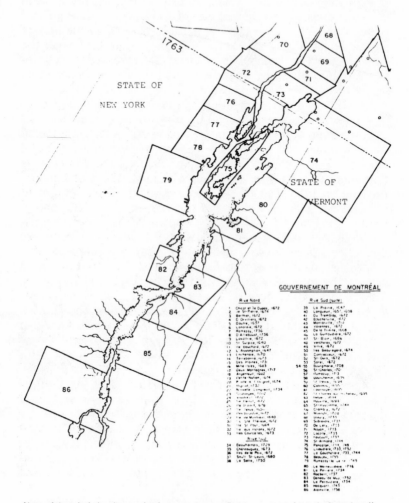

STATE OF
NEW YORK

STATE OF
VERMONT

1763

GOUVERNEMENT DE MONTRÉAL

None of the seigniories shown existed except on paper. Some were granted "at the last minute", e.g.
Alainville (#86) at the north end of what is now called Lake George, New York, in 1758

Continuation of Map no. 75, *Atlas Historique du Canada français*

"Paper" seigniories, New York and Vermont, 1760

Gaspé peninsula, but these areas were not settled during the French Régime. In later years, British settlers usually avoided the seigniories — the Quebec Act of 1774 preserved seigniorial rights along with French law — because they hated the idea of paying feudal dues, a practice that they associated with the detested rents in Scotland and Ireland. However, some seigniories were purchased by Englishmen or Loyalists and opened up for settlement by those who did not mind paying rent.

Perhaps the most important of these "English" seigniories was Beauharnois, near Montreal, which was granted in 1729 and, for some obscure reason, granted again to the same family by King Louis XV in 1750. It was not settled under the Old Régime. The seigniory was sold in 1763 to the Marquis de Lotbinière who, in turn, sold it to Alexander Ellice of London, England, in 1795. Part of the land was surveyed for settlement in 1800 by William Waller and the sections given the names Catherinestown, Helenstown, Annstown,[19] Marystown, Ormstown, Georgetown, and so on, after Ellice's many children. No doubt the suffix "town" was thought to have some appeal to suspicious colonists looking for townships. That is how there came to be some seigniories covered with English place-names. The important seigniory of Chateauguay, part of which is now in suburban Montreal, was barely settled before the English régime. It was then abandoned by its few French-Canadian tenants in the belief that the soil was exhausted. Then it, too, was filled up with English-speaking tenants, to be joined later by new French-Canadian neighbours.

While the seigniorial territory, on which all of the French-Canadians lived, was clearly established as their protected domain, the rest of the new province was thrown open for settlement by all. Counties were named, usually after English or Irish counties or places, and each one divided into townships, as originally decreed in the Royal Proclamation and following the practice in the older, lost, colonies, familiar to the United Empire Loyalists.

Settlers poured in from the United States,[20] Britain and Ireland. In terms of territory, if not of population, Lower

---

[19] Now called Beauharnois; the manor-house (since destroyed by fire) was located there.

[20] Including some Acadians who did not wish to stay in the U.S.A.

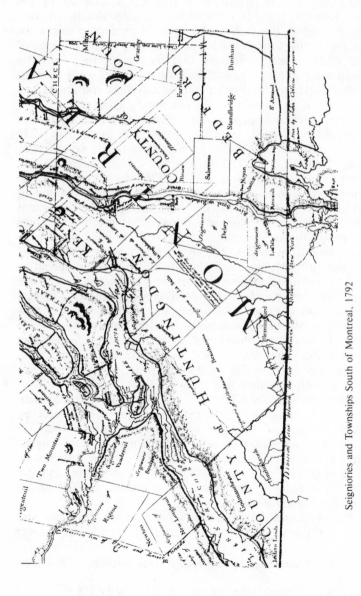

Seigniories and Townships South of Montreal, 1792

Gaspé peninsula, but these areas were not settled during the French Régime. In later years, British settlers usually avoided the seigniories — the Quebec Act of 1774 preserved seigniorial rights along with French law — because they hated the idea of paying feudal dues, a practice that they associated with the detested rents in Scotland and Ireland. However, some seigniories were purchased by Englishmen or Loyalists and opened up for settlement by those who did not mind paying rent.

Perhaps the most important of these "English" seigniories was Beauharnois, near Montreal, which was granted in 1729 and, for some obscure reason, granted again to the same family by King Louis XV in 1750. It was not settled under the Old Régime. The seigniory was sold in 1763 to the Marquis de Lotbinière who, in turn, sold it to Alexander Ellice of London, England, in 1795. Part of the land was surveyed for settlement in 1800 by William Waller and the sections given the names Catherinestown, Helenstown, Annstown,[19] Marystown, Ormstown, Georgetown, and so on, after Ellice's many children. No doubt the suffix "town" was thought to have some appeal to suspicious colonists looking for townships. That is how there came to be some seigniories covered with English place-names. The important seigniory of Chateauguay, part of which is now in suburban Montreal, was barely settled before the English régime. It was then abandoned by its few French-Canadian tenants in the belief that the soil was exhausted. Then it, too, was filled up with English-speaking tenants, to be joined later by new French-Canadian neighbours.

While the seigniorial territory, on which all of the French-Canadians lived, was clearly established as their protected domain, the rest of the new province was thrown open for settlement by all. Counties were named, usually after English or Irish counties or places, and each one divided into townships, as originally decreed in the Royal Proclamation and following the practice in the older, lost, colonies, familiar to the United Empire Loyalists.

Settlers poured in from the United States,[20] Britain and Ireland. In terms of territory, if not of population, Lower

---

[19] Now called Beauharnois; the manor-house (since destroyed by fire) was located there.

[20] Including some Acadians who did not wish to stay in the U.S.A.

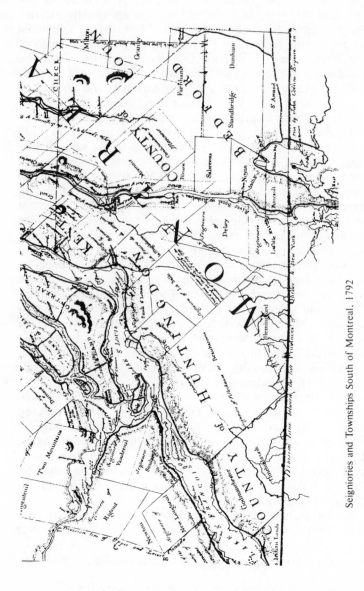

Seigniories and Townships South of Montreal, 1792

From map by Gale and Duberger in the Public Archives of Canada. Map no. 59, *Atlas Historique du Canada français*

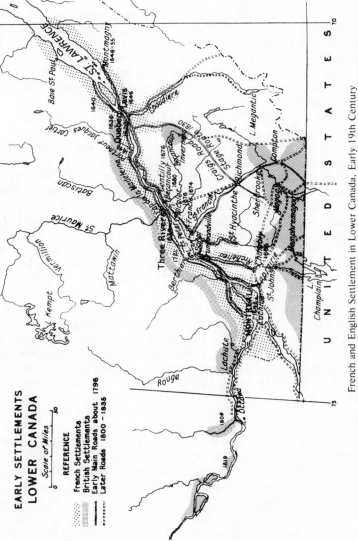

French and English Settlement in Lower Canada, Early 19th Century

Adapted from a map by the Edinburgh Geographical Institute in *Historical Atlas of Canada*, p. 23, No. 62-3, synchronized to ca. 1825

Canada was about as English as it was French. The townships
south of the St Lawrence were in land that was never French
and had no French names at all. In a curious passage, the ultra-
nationalist magazine *La revue indépendantiste*[21] admits that,
after thorough research that even covered "oral" traditions,
Monseigneur Desranleau, Bishop of Sherbrooke, was unable to
uncover evidence that there had ever been a French name for
the Eastern Townships. That disappointment does not prevent
La revue advancing some sort of French prior claim to the area
because it had been "visited", and even "explored" by
Frenchmen. There follows a list of names such as St-Castin and
Rouville, names all too well known in New England because of
the not infrequent massacres by French-led "war-parties". The
French historian Charlevoix described the passage of the war-
parties through the St Francis or Richelieu valleys with rendez-
vous at the White River and then down the Connecticut River
Valley to Deerfield, Massachusetts, which was usually the first
village to "get it in the neck" (or rather, the scalp!) No
mention is made of place-names. The war-parties travelled light
and swept through the winter days on snowshoe, sleeping by
night, huddled together for warmth. With captured New Eng-
landers and booty they hurried home, killing any prisoners who
could not stand the pace. There was obviously no time for, or
inclination to, exploration. Now *La revue indépendantiste*, which
is not coy about the fact that its fanatical partisans have influence with those organs of the Quebec government that operate
the provisions of Bill 101 governing place-names, suggests that
the original English place-names be replaced by contrived
French names, including the names of the leaders of these war-
parties.[22]

By perhaps 1825, with the English-speaking settlement in
the townships and English seigniories and the French-Canadian
population in French seigniorial territory, rural Lower Canada
presented two completely different aspects. One, virtually 100
per cent French, was characterized by richly-decorated Roman
Catholic churches, roadside calvaries and dormer windows on

---

[21] A "true" separatist magazine calling itself "The Voice of the Real
Canada" but which accepts the *Parti Québécois* as a step in the right
direction. Summer, 1978, p. 43.
[22] Summer, 1978, pp. 57-58.

fieldstone houses. The other, virtually 100 per cent English, presented the austere Protestant churches, schoolhouses and red-brick American-style farmhouses. Ignoring the three towns, one could say that Lower Canada might have been two separate colonies, of about equal areas.

Then, beginning in the 1830s and 1840s, a remarkable shift began to take place within the province — a shift that, 140 years later, is still apparently running its course. French-Canadians were leaving the overcrowded seigniories and slowly moving into the English townships. At the same time the English in the townships began to feel the attraction of the growing opportunities in the recently-opened lands of Upper Canada, as well as the professional and commercial attractions in Montreal. That is how Montreal became Canada's third-largest English-speaking city, and how the Eastern Townships have now become more French than English.

The degree to which the French have taken over the townships varies. One county, Brome, continues to have an English majority. Others have thriving English-speaking minorities. Bishop's University at Lennoxville stands as a reminder of this group. In other townships, the English-speaking population is aging, assimilating and slowly disappearing.

Some newer townships were originally proclaimed with English names, but by the time the first settlers arrived the shift of settlement had already begun and they were French from the start. Examples are Bungay, in Kamouraska County, proclaimed in 1863,[23] and Packington, in Témiscouata, in 1869.

South of the St Lawrence the 1850s and 1860s saw the gradual in-filling of the last few unsettled areas, although the Gaspé was not fully opened up until this century. Some townships even received French names, the first being Lessard, in L'Islet county, proclaimed in 1841 (which is remarkable as this was the period of the Durham Report and the sharp anti-French reaction following the rebellion of 1837-38.) By the 1850s and 1860s many new townships were being given French names. The tide of settlement had shifted, and was seen to be shifting.

In most cases, the Roman Catholic Church, anxious to preserve the collective existence of French Canada, organized

---

[23] Apparently surveyed much earlier, as it appears on a map dated 1854.

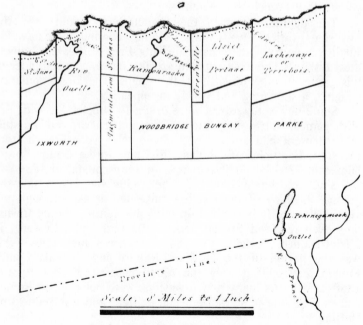

Pattern of Settlement, Kamouraska, 1854

From a Township Survey Map, Province of Canada. From the Map Collection, Department of Rare Books and Special Collections, McGill University Libraries

the "colonization". In 1848, they established at Sherbrooke the *Association des établissements canadiens des townships* (Association of [French-] Canadian Establishments in the Townships). Unsettled land was obtained and farms purchased from departing English. New churches were built, though without the tithing powers that existed in the seigniories. The new young French-Canadian farmers may have been mortgaged to the hilt, but they were the first of their race to own land freely, and their contributions to the church were voluntary. The new communities were named for saints. To prevent confusion, the name of the township was appended, since one could not be sure if the same saint's name did not appear in another part of the province. Thus the origin of those quaint Quebec place-names like Ste-Rosalie-de-Watford, St-Adolphe-de-Dudswell or St-Rémi-de-Tingwick.

Many of the cities and towns of Quebec after the original three — Quebec, Three Rivers and Montreal — were founded by the English-speaking. Sherbrooke and Drummondville are examples. Industry there also began to attract French-Canadians, although the church was uneasy about the trend away from the land. Nevertheless, the absence of seigniorial rules, the new responsibilities of owning land, and the proximity of the English-speaking as neighbours and as employers, suppliers or customers, led to a broadening of outlook among the French-Canadians in the townships.

For over 100 years the French-Canadian outlook in the townships has been broad, conservative and wary of radicalism, yet very much in favour of good relations with English Canada, learning English, and all the many things that are anathema to separatists. Even in 1976 the *Parti Québécois* won very few seats in the rural townships. Co-author William Shaw likes to remember the warm reception that he and Bryce Mackasey received during Canada Week celebrations at Bury, in Compton County, where many residents cannot even speak English. It is not uncommon for French-Canadians living in the townships to declare publicly by means of signed letters to the press that if Quebec were ever to separate from Canada they would move to another province, even though they would have to learn English.

This open attitude of the French-Canadians in the townships leads us to believe that, just as in the case of the native people in Rupert's Land, the majority of the French-speaking population south of the St Lawrence, and virtually all of the English-speaking population in the area, would wish to remain in Canada. They would lend even more weight to Canada's insistence that this region not be given to the foreign country that the separatists wish to establish.

Generally, the peaceful movement of the French-Canadians into the townships was neither welcomed nor opposed by the original English-speaking inhabitants. The tone of the comment made by the editor of the Huntingdon *Gleaner* in 1875 describes the situation: "My story is of the chief settlement in Quebec of Old Country immigrants, of their struggles, their trials, and their triumphs in subduing an inhospitable tract of country, and of their relations with the French-Canadian people, amidst whom they exist like a sand bank in the sea, always threatened with overflow and extinction, yet unmoved by the surrounding waters."[24]

Ultra-nationalist teachers and propagandists like to seize on the rare evidence of opposition to the French newcomers and present it in such a way as to make it appear that there were major obstacles placed by the English inhabitants and landowners. For example a certain Judge Sewell, in 1810, suggested the anglicization of Quebec by means of heavy immigration from the British Isles. From the way in which this obscure official is quoted, one would think that Sewell had been a major figure in history. *La revue indépendantiste* (Summer 1978) mentions a "No Frenchman need apply" rule as having been in existence, but offers no evidence. The flat statement is made that "The French-Canadians only penetrated the Eastern Townships after 1850," as if some long, arduous struggle to open the gates had been needed. The census figures of per cent French-Canadian population for the Eastern Townships counties read as follows:

---

²⁴   *The History of the County of Huntingdon*, p. 2.

County	1844	1851-2
Beauharnois*	42.5	49.4
Drummond	59.8	68.9
Mégantic	38.0	60.9
Missisquoi	13.7	19.5
Shefford	28.5	44.2
Stanstead	5.3	9.3

*Beauharnois County was then half seigniorial and half township, including the present Huntingdon.

It is an oddity of modern politics and ideology that, with this historical background, French-Canadian ultra-nationalists refer to the English of Quebec as *intruders*. Even René Lévesque, who considers himself an "honest fellow" says of his birthplace in Cox Township:

"New Carlisle was initially settled by Loyalists who entrenched themselves there and they had all the power. They weren't evil people: they simply treated the French-Canadians the way the white Rhodesians treat their blacks."[25]

Surely Lévesque knows that this statement, with its insulting innuendo, is based on pure invention. The whites conquered the territory of the Rhodesian tribes and pushed them out of the choicest lands, allowing them to re-enter them only under the most servile conditions. The Quebec English settled only the townships land, which had never been French, and not only granted the right of the French on their traditional lands in the seigniories but allowed them to move freely into the English lands and take them over. The Lévesques moved into Cox Township, which French-Canadians are now taking over by sheer weight of numbers, as free men in full possession of their franchise as Canadians, politically equal to all other Canadians.

In the planning of Confederation, English rural Quebec was ably represented by Alexander Galt of Sherbrooke. It was recognized that the English in the proposed new province to be named Quebec would be a minority. To give them some protection, the British North America Act contains several provisions, including one that specifically sets out that each of the then

[25] Hélène Pilotte, *Châtelaine* magazine, April, 1966, quoted in *René Lévesque* etc., p. 14 (Eng. ed.).

English counties would have one representative in the legislature of Quebec, regardless of shifts of population. At that time it was not thought that the French would continue to move into the townships and the English out, to the point that most of the "guaranteed" English counties became French. Their guaranteed representation no longer has any significance and the relevant section of the B.N.A. Act has been repealed. Nevertheless, Confederation, which is the only source of authority of the Canadian government, intended that the English territory in Quebec be protected. No Canadian government has the right, therefore, to give the English territory of Quebec to a foreign country.

Historically, the constitutionally-protected English territory of Quebec is based on the Eastern Townships and the Ottawa Valley. (That particular provision did not extend to the "northern townships" or the Gaspé or the Gulf North Shore.) However, with the shift of population, the present territory of the English of Quebec is only partly in the formerly protected regions. The majority of Anglo-Quebeckers now live on the archipelago of Montreal, and their rights, together with the rights of the English-speaking population north of the St Lawrence, are the subject of the next chapter.

6

The Myth of Entitlement: "Federalist" Quebec

The part of Quebec south of Rupert's Land but north of the St Lawrence river and gulf, including the islands of the Montreal archipelago, would have remained French if France had accepted Sir Thomas Robinson's final proposal of 1755. This part had been conceded as French on Mitchell's authoritative map of that year. Even Huske's map, which was more assertive in its definition of the Iroquois lands that were conceded as being under British hegemony by the Treaty of Utrecht, would only take from the part of Quebec in question the triangle of territory enclosed between the Ottawa and St Lawrence rivers, now the counties of Vaudreuil and Soulanges. Therefore, from a diplomatic and legal point of view, this territory, still vast, could be that of an independent French state. But in terms of original settlement, much of this territory was not French.

Just as there are "Eastern" townships, so are there "northern" townships, stretching in a tier across the Laurentians that ends just behind Quebec City. Most of the Ottawa Valley also consists of townships. All of them have a legitimate English character because they were originally settled by the English-speaking and, in several cases, they still have English-speaking majorities or sizeable minorities.

Some 150 years ago, Richard Joy writes in the *American Review of Canadian Studies*, "English was the language most commonly spoken in the Eastern Townships of Quebec, on both sides of the Ottawa Valley and even in the foothills of the Laurentians, north of Quebec City (in many of these areas, Gaelic was the second language and French ran a poor third). At the census immediately preceding Confederation, persons of French origin were a minority at Montreal and made up barely 20 per cent of what is now the metropolitan area of Hull.["]

[1] "Languages in Conflict, 1976" (article), Autumn, 1976.

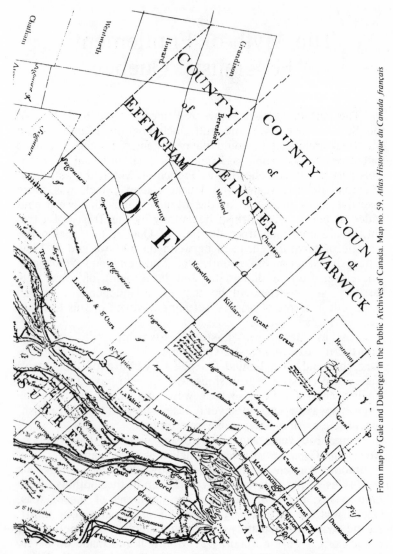

Seigniories and Townships, North of the St Lawrence, 1792

The early English-speaking settlement in many of the northern townships soon gave way to French newcomers. Priests such as Father Provost worked tirelessly and heroically to urge the French-Canadians to save themselves from the effects of overpopulation and from the horrors of emigration to the United States — the land of assimilation.

An excerpt from Father Provost's rhetoric gives us a good idea of the spirit behind the French "takeover" of the northern townships and is equally illuminating as far as the Eastern Townships are concerned.

> " . . . inquire around the great parishes ranged along the edge of the mountains as to the value to their shopkeepers and professionals of the townships of Rawdon, Chertsey, Kildare, Cathcart and the parish of St-Jean-de-Matha[2] — also situated in the mountains . . . Language, laws, moral outlook, and customs, in other words nationality, are protected. . . For we would search in vain the means, even the feasibility, of preserving ourselves, if we did not seize the territory that is available to us in the townships of the north and of the south." Then, urging his listeners to spread the word, he criticized the *habitants*: " . . . as long as they have a few *piastres* ("bucks") left they stubbornly remain on parcels of land that are too small, and it is only after spending their last shilling that they finally make up their minds to follow the road to the townships."[3]

The priests like Father Provost, who led the colonization of the townships of Quebec by diverting French-Canadians who would otherwise have emigrated, deserve the gratitude of all Canada, both English and French.

While the townships northeast of Montreal have become heavily French, those in the Ottawa Valley, including the Gatineau and other valleys tributary to the Ottawa, and many stretching along the Ontario border up to Timiskaming, still have thriving English-speaking communities. One county has an

---

[2] Located in an inland extension to one of the seigniories.
[3] Report in *L'Union des cantons de l'est* (newspaper), January 10, 1867.

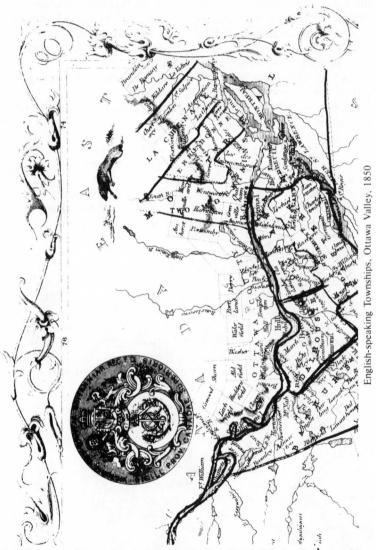

English-speaking Townships, Ottawa Valley, 1850

Detail from a map of Canada West drawn by J. Rapkin. From the Map Collection, Department of Rare Books and Special Collections, McGill University Libraries

English-speaking majority, and others have English-majority townships. The anti-separatist "Quebec-Canada Movement" was launched in Aylmer, in the Ottawa Valley. As in the townships south of the St Lawrence, so in the townships of the Ottawa Valley[4] the sentiment and determination to remain in Canada are very strong.

There is also a special reason why the people of the city of Hull, mostly Francophone, have a strong desire to remain part of Canada: they believe that their region benefits from its proximity to Ottawa, just across the river. The presence of huge Federal goverment offices in Hull, and the expensive public works carried out by the Federal government throughout the National Capital Region, which includes Hull and its suburbs, are a daily testimony to a strong job-creating Federal presence. In a way, Hull has been "bought" by Canada. It is a transaction of which the authors do not particularly approve. Nevertheless it is a fact.

Hull's M.P., Dr Gaston Isabelle, has been campaigning for years to have Hull and its suburbs included in his proposed new Federal district, to be modelled on the District of Columbia and which would be neither part of Ontario nor part of Quebec. "Hull and Western Quebec" says Dr Isabelle "would never go along with independence. If Quebec could separate from Canada, the region known as the *Outaouais* (the Ottawa Valley) could separate from Quebec and join with the Federal district." Reporter Gillian Cosgrove found "Most residents interviewed at random on the streets . . . in favour of a federal district. Marc Cayer, 43, of Lucerne echoed the sentiments of many when he said: 'If Quebec can decide to separate by a referendum, why can't we? If democracy works in Quebec, it should work for the people of the *Outaouais* too."[5] While Miss Cosgrove did not take the Federal district idea very seriously and found some opposition to it, it was clear that the desire to stay part of Canada was very strong.

The upper part of the region, which includes the part of the Abitibi district that happens to lie outside of Rupert's Land, is also concerned about the danger of being separated from

---

[4] There are also some seigniories in the Ottawa Valley, settled long after the Conquest. One of them was the fief of Papineau.

[5] *The Montreal Star*, December 31, 1976.

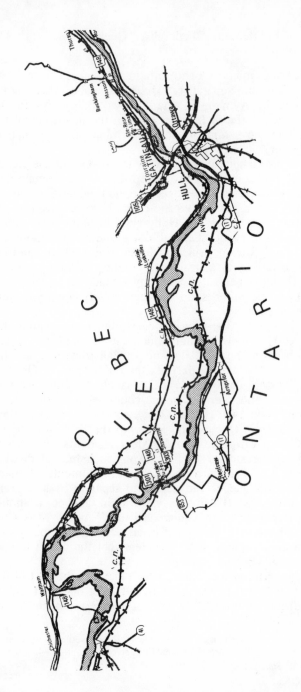

Cross-Border Transport Routes, Ottawa-Pembroke

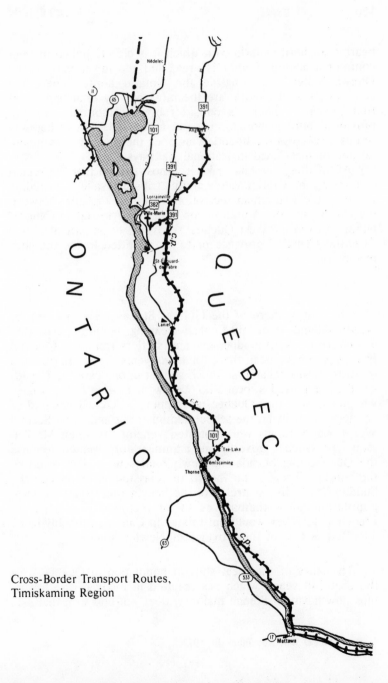

Cross-Border Transport Routes,
Timiskaming Region

nearby northern Ontario with which it is closely linked in their common isolation. Both this area, and the lower part of the Ottawa Valley, lie alongside the Ontario border where the adjacent parts of Ontario are the most heavily Francophone of that province. There is considerable intercourse over the provincial border, both social and commercial. Busy highway routes criss-cross the boundary as does the main transcontinental line of the Canadian National Railways.

All of these reasons make it almost certain that the region comprising the Ottawa Valley and its tributary valleys, including much of the Laurentian recreation area, and the area between the Ottawa and the Abitibi region, would opt to stay in Canada, either to form a "West Quebec" province or as part of a new "Central Canada" province or to be admitted to the province of Ontario.

The North Shore of the Gulf of St Lawrence, adjacent to Newfoundland, is mainly English-speaking, being populated by a mixture of Newfoundlanders and settlers from the Channel Islands who have been there for many years. They are oriented towards Newfoundland, so much so that in one case the Canadian Press reported a local who "knew of no one in the village who subscribed to a Quebec newspaper . . . A villager told of an incident involving the school administrator and some Second World War veterans who protested vehemently when Mr Poisson [the Quebec government administrator] wanted to raise the Quebec flag outside the newly-built school. The result of the conflict: There is no flag in the classrooms or outside the building."[6] — By no stretch of the imagination would the local population allow themselves to be included in a separate French state. They would opt to stay in Canada, probably to be admitted as part of the province of Newfoundland.

The story of the great shift in population in Quebec over the past 140 years, which has resulted in many of the townships now having a French majority, does not end with that side

---

[6] *The Montreal Star*, November 30, 1977.

of the coin. During the same period, the English-speaking have taken over parts of the seigniorial territory. These areas, in the Montreal archipelago, are of lesser size than the townships that were abandoned, but they are wealthier and more populous. How these areas came to be English-speaking is part of the story.

At the time of the British Conquest, the newly-installed English-speaking civilian population consisted of a few dozen British officials, and a handful of traders from England and from the older British colonies, including some Jewish merchants from the West Indies and from England. This tiny population was spread among the three little towns, Quebec City, Three Rivers and Montreal. We say "little" because at that time the cities of the other British provinces were quite large. Philadelphia was then the second-largest English-speaking city in the world. The entire population of the new province could just fill a few counties in New York or Massachusetts.

In the three towns the English-speaking traders at first clamoured for the full range of British laws and an elected assembly, which they would have controlled since the French-Canadians, as Roman Catholics, would have had no vote. The merchants expected the small French population to be engulfed in a wave of English-speaking settlement on the scale known in the other colonies to the south. Particularly in Montreal, away from the scrutiny of the Governor, many of the traders from the southern provinces were openly revolutionary in their attitude. Montreal even voted to send two "representatives" to the Continental Congress in Philadelphia.[7]

However, Britain, which early on saw the advantages of befriending the French-Canadians (a personal interest of the King himself), passed the Quebec Act in 1774. The Roman Catholic religion and the seigniorial rules, along with French civil law generally, were given a privileged position, unique in the British Empire. In England itself Roman Catholics could not then vote or hold public office. Indirectly, these provisions gave a semi-official status to the French language which was used by ecclesiastical bodies and in the civil "courts of com-

---

[7] In the event, one merchant, James Price, went to Philadelphia as an informal representative. *Montreal, The Days That* etc., p. 50.

mon pleas". It was in any case the practice to make important official documents available in French as well as English.

The main purpose of these privileges was to inoculate French Canada against the revolutionary infection, and in this it apparently succeeded. Even though the revolutionaries occupied Montreal, and Benjamin Franklin sojourned there, sponsoring Fleury Mesplet in the founding of *The Gazette* and bringing Father Carroll from Baltimore to try to persuade the French-Canadian clergy to support them, they were eventually forced to return south empty-handed, leaving the British once more in control of Canada.

The English-speaking merchants in the three towns[8] prospered alongside their French-Canadian competitors. The English-speaking, being few, were forced to learn French in order to get along, which they accepted with good grace once they realized that the Quebec Act was there to stay. Many married French-Canadian girls. *The Gazette* reverted to publishing in French only. The merchants dawdled or slept during the winter months until the St Lawrence thawed sufficiently to allow the new season's trading to begin.

It was in the late 1790s and the early 1800s that Montreal's great "natural resources", the Lachine Rapids, which prevented ocean-going vessels plying further inland, and the confluence of the St Lawrence and Ottawa rivers, which placed the town at the start of the canoe route to the northern and western portions of Rupert's Land and the North-west Territory, began to have a wondrous effect. The fur trade started to grow at a rapid rate, and became "big business". The Montreal fur traders, the Scotch in the lead, but with the active participation of Jews such as Henry Joseph,[9] explored ever

----

[8] But Samuel Jacobs, a maverick Jewish trader, lived at St-Denis on the Richelieu and carried on his many businesses from there.

[9] Joseph's brilliant career (he was dubbed the "founder of the Canadian Merchant Marine") outshone that of two earlier Montreal Jews, whose participation in the fur trade was at a somewhat earthier level. In 1778, the fledgling Spanish & Portuguese Synagogue, Canada's first, adopted a "code" whose obvious purpose was to pressure these "wandering fur Jews" to sign up. But some managed their own rules as is clear from the "code" as finally promulgated: "Any Israelite that will not sign these our laws and regulations (that are inhabitants of this town) within twenty days, and those out of town (temporarily), within six months, shall for

further. In 1793 Alexander Mackenzie, followed by Simon Fraser in 1808, opened up active all-British fur trading routes to the Pacific coast. Montreal began to change. More ambitious Scotchmen and Englishmen arrived and, supported by the new hinterland in the townships to the south and west and trade with the Loyalist settlements in Upper Canada, the English-speaking community was now big enough to stand on its own, to support its own newspapers and to pass through the process that rapidly led to the founding of the Bank of Montreal in 1817 and McGill University in 1821.

The situation between English and French in Montreal altered. "In 1779" as Hilda Neatby says "there had appeared the first of a series of agreements associating a number of individuals engaged in the fur trade, under the name of the North West Company. The company included some of the greatest names in the later fur trade: Joseph and Benjamin Frobisher, Simon McTavish and James McGill. The agreements helped to eliminate wasteful and violent competition and to regulate the relations between wintering partners, Montreal agents, and London merchants, which grew ever more complicated as the trade lines lengthened. The advent of the large company saw the beginning of the end of the equal and friendly association of English and and [French-] Canadians in the fur trade. The English almost from the beginning had been the larger investors, but a merchant was in the trade whether he sent one or twenty canoes up country. The appearance of the large and powerful company, with a limited number of shares all held by individuals or firms active in the trade, tended to eliminate Canadians from this aspect of the enterprise. Of well-known Canadian names in the trade only one, Maurice Regis Blondeau, appeared among the North Westers before 1791; another, Charles Chaboillez, came in 1794. There were several

---

ever be exempted from having any privilege, honour or employment in this congregation, and be looked on as no member thereof, except only Chapman Abraham (usually at Detroit) and Benjamin Lyon (usually at Michilimackinac) who are at too great a distance, but allowing them twenty days after their arrival in this town." (Quoted by Stuart Rosenberg, *The Jewish Community in Canada* from the *Minutes of the Spanish and Portuguese Congregation of Montreal* in the American Jewish Archives, Cincinnati. Rabbi Rosenberg's book is our source for the other references in this chapter to early Jewish history.)

reasons for the absence of Canadian names. Canadians had less capital; they tended to prefer a one-man or family business; and the strong instinct for family property made them shun the heavy financial risks involved in trade in the far northwest."[10]

Not everyone would agree with Dr Neatby's explanation, but whatever the reason, between 1790 and 1820, Montreal changed into a pushing, growing, English-speaking city. Towards the end of that period the English-speaking merchant element in the town of Three Rivers, led by the sons of Aaron Hart, one of the pioneers of Jewish settlement in Canada, gradually moved to Montreal. Three Rivers reverted to being French, as it is today.

Quebec City's English-speaking population was less purely mercantile than that of Montreal, since the town was also the seat of government for Quebec, and then of Lower Canada. Later it alternated with Toronto as the capital of the united province of Canada. The latter role continued until about 1860 when the Civil Service began to move to Ottawa, the new "neutral" capital. Quebec City was also the main point of entry for British immigrants, especially after Governor Sir James Craig ordered construction of his road from Lévis to Richmond. The English-speaking and the French-Canadian merchants of Quebec City tended to be more equal in their wealth and influence. They prospered on the development of the Quebec hinterland through the forest industries and later through ship-building. By the 1860s the English-speaking were about 40 per cent of the population, the Upper Town was a mixed English and French area and Quebec still was larger than Toronto.

Then, quite suddenly, the English-speaking population of Quebec City declined to the point where, from the census of 1861 to that of 1871, the total population of the town actually decreased. Not only did the departure of Canadian civil servants for Ottawa, and of the British garrison for home, reduce the employment available, but also Quebec City could not compete with the opportunities springing up in Montreal and Toronto. Moreover, the Quebec provincial Civil Service gradually became less English. As described elsewhere, the

---

[10] *Quebec: The Revolutionary Age*, pp. 219-220.

province's Civil Service today is over 98 per cent French-Canadian. The English-speaking community there has dwindled and is on the point of extinction. So Quebec City has joined Three Rivers in reverting to being completely French.

Montreal's wealth grew rapidly because the city was a major entrepôt (receiving, storage and forwarding centre). After 1850, industries associated with its entrepôt nature began to spring up. Eventually the pool of labour, skills and wealth led to a growing manufacturing industry. Finally, after 1890, Montreal matured into a major financial centre with head offices of major Canadian and multi-national corporations. At first, the pool of labour was filled by immigration from Great Britain and Ireland. By 1840 Montreal had an English-speaking, and largely British-born, majority. But, after 1865, the stream of British immigration was outnumbered by migration of French-Canadians escaping over-population in the seigniorial countryside. Even the new immigration from the European continent did not keep pace.

By 1890 the French-Canadians were again the numerical majority in Montreal, but they were for the most part poor and lived in densely-populated pockets in the city. Moreover, the church authorities were very concerned about the effects of city life and did their best to make the local parish, rather than the workplace or the city, the centre of social existence. Family ties remained very strong, and Montreal had for many years almost no violent crime. What little there was seldom involved French-Canadians.

Thus, while its French-speaking majority was, as it still is, about 65 per cent of the population, Montreal became, if anything, even more "British". As recently as the 1930s and 1940s Union Jacks flew from almost every perch. It is hard to imagine any city in the world with more places and institutions named after Queen Victoria: several Victoria streets and avenues, Victoria Square, Victoria Pier, Victoria Jubilee Bridge, the Queen's Jubilee Laundry Company (its vans were a frequent sight, bearing imposing portraits of Queen Victoria on either side), Royal Victoria Hospital and Royal Victoria College, to name some.

Only on certain holidays, such as St John the Baptist or Corpus Christi, would French-Canadian parades take over the

Unilingual English signs, Dorchester Street, Montreal, 1953
Desjardins' famous restaurant is now situated on Mackay Street.

Photo courtesy of Mme Lorraine Desjardins

main streets, flying the Vatican flag. On Sundays, French-Canadian Catholicism would "conquer" the sound waves of Montreal as the lovely and evocative church bells rang out to summon the faithful to the frequent and well-attended masses. This is not to say that Montreal's institutions were all English. The civic administration was bilingual, and most official signs were in both languages except in some English-speaking districts and "downtown" where occasionally only the English version was used. The more technical side of the local administration tended to be unilingual English. One still sees metal covers engraved "MWW" ("Montreal Water Works"). The courts, with the legal and notarial professions, were about equally French and English, with a high degree of bilingualism among the English-speaking lawyers and notaries.

While French-Canadian influence on Montreal's architecture was considerable, everything to do with business, technology and modern communications was then almost entirely in English. Even retail trade was conducted mostly in English. Up to 1960 Montreal was consciously the metropolis of Canada. It was where men (and wives) climbing the ladder of business and social success reached the top. A typical attitude is revealed in the case of Sir Edward Beatty, then plain Beatty:

"The move from Toronto to Montreal brought about many changes in Beatty himself. Hitherto he had led the easy life of a youngest son with no responsibilities and little work, a comfortable home and plenty of sport; now he found himself in a rooming house with an occupation which tied him to an office stool all day . . . From the beginning of his stay at Mrs Cassidy's he made it plain that success was his major objective in life . . . The young sportsman from Toronto had been transformed, almost overnight, into the prodigiously hard worker who was ultimately to become one of the busiest men in Canada."[11]

Montreal looked outward over all of Canada, from the landing of a winter cargo at Halifax to the sale of a life insurance policy in Victoria. Sir William Van Horne would tell his visitors that through the window of his office in Montreal he

---

[11] *Beatty of the C.P.R.*, pp. 21-22. The "rooming house" was of a high class, and a necessity for a respectable bachelor.

would see, not the rooftops and spires of Montreal, but the Pacific Ocean.

All of this took place in the English language. In fact, that is still the case although many firms are reluctant to admit the fact because of current political pressures. The English-speaking character of Montreal has a strong bearing on the character of the territory of greater Montreal, particularly the western part of the islands of Montreal and Jésus, and Ile Perrot.

Under the French régime, Montreal lived very much within its walls, crammed into narrow streets. The Gentlemen of St-Sulpice, a kind of priestly order of laymen, had been granted the seigniorial title to the whole island outside of the little town, but there were few settlements. The same sparseness of settlement existed on the other islands of the archipelago of Montreal and on the south shore of the St Lawrence. The desire to stay close together and to avoid exposure to Indian attacks resulted in the existence of a vast tract of empty land all around the walls. With the coming of the English, Montreal expanded outside its walls, beginning symbolically with the garrison encamping to the west near what is now McGill Street.

Later, along the north wall, Peter McGill and other citizens organized the in-filling of a flood stream and called it Craig Street. In general, to the west and north of the walls of old Montreal, the residents, the businesses, the original surveying and naming of streets, in short everything about the central-western part of what is now the centre of the city, was English-speaking. (Even today, despite the current attempt to eliminate English street names by "consolidation", there are few French names on streets or squares or business houses in the western commercial heart of Montreal). When Ignace Bourget, Bishop of Montreal, (who is said to have originated the maxim 'Speak English but speak it badly') proposed that the new Roman Catholic cathedral be erected on its present site on Dominion Square he was bitterly criticized by many French-Canadians for placing the church in the English part of the city.

Early in the 19th century, the English-speaking began to build summer residences on and around the mountain that now stands in the middle of the city, and later in the century, along the "Lakeshore" in the western part of the island. The city grew by annexation and by new suburbs, such as Westmount. The new suburbs were English-speaking with the exception of

Outremont (literally "beyond the mountain"), which began life as a fashionable place for the French-speaking élite.

In this century summer residences gave way to suburban development, virtually 100 per cent English-speaking to the west and mainly English-speaking in other directions, as railway services, and, later, modern roads, made commuting practical. By this time, the summer residents on the mountain had been bought out and Mount Royal Park completed to the design of Frederick Olmstead, the creator of New York's Central Park.

Usually, where there was no existing settlement or place-name, the new suburb would be given an English name such as Montreal West, Town of Mount Royal, or Greenfield Park. In some cases a French name of the local natural feature was adapted as the name of the town, as in the case of Baie-d'Urfé, a suburb that has always been almost purely English-speaking. Often, a small French settlement was engulfed by English development, but the French name and old French village centre remain, whether as a municipality or as part of a larger city. Co-author Shaw is the member of the Quebec legislature for Pointe-Claire, originally settled in 1713 but now so English that most of its residents do not even know what "Pointe-Claire" means ("bright point"). They shop along "Sources Road" not knowing that it means "springs road".

Hundreds of thousands of English-speaking Montrealers have probably never stopped to think that their familiar St Antoine Street really means "St Anthony Street" or that mainly-English "N.D.G." (nicknamed "No Damned Good"), which stands for *Notre-Dame-de-Grâce* would be, with equal irreverence, "O.L.G." ("Our Lady of Grace") if it were translated into their own language. In most cases, in the traditional Quebec manner, the two language groups informally agree on one name, except for a handful of street names such as St James which is *St-Jacques* in the original French usage. Laziness helps. English-speaking Montrealers say "peenuff" for "Pie IX Boulevard", even if they literally cannot even count up to ten in French. So much easier than trying to say "Pius the Ninth Boulevard", with two extra syllables!

The English-speaking takeover of originally "French" territory around Montreal, beginning in 1840 and continuing to this day, is matched in these same characteristics, and over the same span of years, by the French-speaking takeover of "En-

glish" territory in the townships and "English" seigniories.
Young French-Canadians in Sherbrooke meet for coffee on *la
rue King*, not thinking or caring that in French it would be *la
rue du Roi*. Not many of Valleyfield's 25,000 citizens know
what either "valley" or "field" mean in their own language.
These everyday realities illustrate the effects of the vast demo-
graphic shift that has taken place in Quebec. They also demonstrate that the separatists can try to argue from historical right,
or they can try to argue from present possession. But they
cannot argue both ways at the same time.

The English-speaking character of central and western
Montreal and Jésus islands is reflected in its strong pro-Canad-
ian outlook. Even in their 1976 sweep the *Parti Québécois* lost
in all but five[12] of the 18 seats in that area, and often ran a
poor third. The population of the central and western half of
the Montreal archipelago would opt to stay in Canada.

This territory in Montreal is not essential to the economy
of independent Laurentia.[13] The "natural resources" of the
Lachine Rapids and the confluence of the St Lawrence and
Ottawa rivers no longer have any significance. The real wealth
of Montreal is due to its position in the Canadian economy.
Take Montreal out of Canada and it would quickly die. It is
dying slowly now because the ultra-nationalist policies of successive Quebec governments since 1960 have partly isolated
Montreal's business community from the rest of Canada, using
language regulations, and referendums, as the barrier.

In fact, a separate French-Canadian state would be much
better off economically if it did not include central and western
Montreal! This paradox is explained simply by the fact that
with Montreal still in Canada, and *ipso facto* exempt from
Laurentia's language laws, the city would resume its economic
growth. Should there be a genuine "association" between Laurentia and Canada, with reasonably free passage of goods and

---

[12] Fabre, L'Acadie, Crémazie, St-Henri, Ste-Anne. Only in Crémazie which
is on the "border" did they come close to winning in 1973 when separatism was the issue. In a 1979 by-election in D'Arcy McGee riding in the
west end of Montreal the Liberal candidate received over 99% of the vote
and the *Parti Québécois* less than 1%. This demonstrates the potential for
partition of Montreal; and, its obverse, the impossibility of including
central and western Montreal in a separate French state.

[13] A name for the separate French state.

persons, Montreal would provide hundreds of thousands of jobs and a handy market for citizens and products from nearby Laurentia. The eastern part of Montreal would be in Laurentia, with only French schools and signs, and so on, allowed.

It is incidental that Montreal is even in the province of Quebec. In 1774 the province stretched from the Gulf of St Lawrence to the Mississippi Valley, including Montreal and what is now southern Ontario. In 1791, what was left of the province of Quebec after the American Revolution was split into two provinces, Upper Canada, now Ontario, and Lower Canada, now Quebec. In 1841, those two provinces were reunited in the single province of Canada.

During the deliberations leading up to Confederation, John Sandfield Macdonald (not to be confused with Sir John A. Macdonald), member of the assembly for Cornwall, former Prime Minister, and later to become the first Premier of Ontario, tended for a time to favour dividing the old province of Canada into three provinces instead of two. The third province would have stretched from the river Trent on the west (Peterborough), or possibly from Belleville, to Montreal on the east, possibly to include the Eastern Townships.[14] This region or future province was called "Central Canada", a name still used in the title of the annual exhibition at Ottawa. Sandfield Macdonald's concerns were that central Canada (mainly what is now eastern Ontario) would suffer neglect if it were combined in the same province with the Lake Peninsula, and that it needed to be firmly bound to its port and natural centre of Montreal. He feared that the Ottawa-Cornwall-Belleville area would be cut off from Montreal by the type of provincial border restraints that had been in force when there were the two provinces.[15] (Little could he have

---

[14] It was Montreal's *The Gazette* that suggested the alternative limits.

[15] "Will the people of Central Canada consent to be thus cut off from their market? To Montreal we send our grain, our timber, our ashes. From Montreal we obtain our money. From Upper Canada we only get bad law and worse chancery . . . No, our interests are with the East, and perhaps the best solution of the difficulty, if it were pressed much further, would be found in carrying the Province line west to the Trent." — Report by the *Daily Leader,* June 19, 1861, quoted by W. L. Morton in *The Critical Years.* Historian Morton does not give a favourable overall opinion of Sandfield Macdonald's abilities and it is perhaps owing to those shortcomings that the "Central Canada" idea never figured in Confederation as eventually developed.

imagined the new twists now thought up, such as restrictions on construction trades working across provincial boundaries!)

In those days, too, Glengarry, the easternmost county in what is now Ontario, and Huntingdon, now in the southwest corner of Quebec, had very close ties. The two counties face each other across the widening of the St Lawrence called Lake St Francis, although there are some stepping-stone islands near Cornwall. At that time, the two counties, with their many Scotch families related to each other, maintained contact by boat in the summer and over the ice in the winter. Today, in the automotive age, contacts between the two counties are less direct because the shortest road route is *via* the United States. However, as a vestige of this past closeness, the Cornwall television station is popular in Huntingdon County.

Looking back, Sandfield Macdonald's third province has many attractions. Central Canada would now be about half French and half English, making a good pivot for the whole country. Eastern Ontario is not a very prosperous region, despite the bonanza of having the swollen Ottawa bureaucracy in its midst.

But no matter how attractive it would be to have Montreal's commercial heart and western districts in Canada, few separatists would wish it. The realities of the economic world are very far from the thoughts of ultra-nationalist politicians. "Anti-business attitudes" wrote Dominique Clift "are deeply rooted among some sections of French Quebec. Nobody was taken by surprise when [then] Financial Institutions Minister Lise Payette said recently of a group of businessmen she was about to meet 'these are not the sort of people whom I usually go out of my way to meet.' The feeling that businessmen, because of their regular contacts with English-speaking people, are somehow culturally alien is quite prevalent in the Parti Québécois."[16] Rodrigue Tremblay, in his letter of resignation from the Lévesque government, said " . . . the cabinet did not include any businessmen and, in fact, very few people with any contacts with the economic milieu of production."[17]

Far from appreciating that most of Montreal's wealth derives from its position as a centre of Canada's business, trans-

---

[16]   *The Montreal Star*, June 9, 1977.
[17]   *The Montreal Star*, September 22, 1979.

port, and communications, and also as an important regional centre for eastern Ontario and western Quebec togther (just as in Sandfield Macdonald's time), the ultra-nationalists see its wealth as somehow being generated internally, almost out of thin air, or out of local business within the province. While there are a few big enterprises in Montreal that have substantial markets in Quebec, the great majority operate all over Canada, and abroad, to the extent that the Quebec market, for many, is less than 10 per cent of the whole.

There are civil servants and politicians in Quebec who privately admit that the English-speaking are the motor or wealth-generators of Montreal because of their ties with the English-speaking outside world. Yet they believe that the main body of English would stay, despite Bill 22, Bill 101, and new constitutional arrangements be they called "sovereignty-association" or something else. Some hark back to the period after 1774 when the English in Montreal complained bitterly about the Quebec Act. After all, Bill 22, Bill 101, and perhaps even a mild dose of "sovereignty-association" could be thought of as logical, if extreme, extensions of the Quebec Act. If the Montreal English managed to adapt to the Quebec Act, then, it is reasoned, their 1980 counterparts could and would adapt to "sovereignty-association". These notions are not realistic. In 1774 it paid the English-speaking merchants to stay because of the city's geographical advantages. Those advantages no longer exist. It does not pay to stay. The exodus, begun in 1960, goes on and on.

We can summarize the outcome of the hypothetical negotiation of sovereignty as follows: — The part of Rupert's Land in Quebec would become the North-East Territories of Canada. — The part of Quebec south of the St Lawrence River would remain Canadian, either as part of a new province, or with the Gaspé admitted to New Brunswick and the balance with "West Quebec". — The Ottawa Valley, including its tributary valleys in the Laurentians, and the Timiskaming district up to and

The Outcome of Negotiations

including the part of the Abitibi district not in Rupert's Land, would stay in Canada, either as a new province of "West Quebec", or admitted to Ontario, or as part of a "Central Canada" province. — The North Shore of the Gulf of St Lawrence would stay in Canada, probably to be admitted to Newfoundland. — The central and western part of the archipelago of Montreal would stay in Canada, to be part of "West Quebec", or as part of Ontario, or in "Central Canada".

The rest of the province of Quebec would cease to be a part of Canada, and would become an independent country called, let us say, "Laurentia". It would be a sizeable country, and would have, barring cross-migration or transfers, a population of about 2,900,000, of which about 2,825,000 would be Francophone.[18] Such a country, in a free trade association with Canada, would be in an excellent economic position. The main drawback would be that during its formative years it would be in the hands of rigid, bureaucratic élitist intellectuals who would gradually extinguish freedom and democracy.

The Zionists dreamt for years of establishing a National Home for the Jews in Palestine. Every Jewish household had its little blue box for donations to the Jewish National Fund to purchase land there. On the box was a map of Palestine. In 1948 the dream of the Zionists came true, except for the map. Palestine was partitioned; but the Zionists were content. The *Parti Québécois* has many ardent separatists in its ranks. They are as passionately devoted to their cause as the Zionists to theirs. Many of them would, if "push comes to shove", accept partition.

Back to reality. Such a country will not be proclaimed — ever. The French-Canadian people would not have it. *They would rather have a large province than a small country.* That is why separation will not happen.

---

[18] The parts remaining in Canada would then contain 2,000,000 Francophones and 1,100,000 non-Francophones. We should also mention that, instead of negotiating over the partition of Quebec, Canada need only make use of the right of any country to excise territory that it does not want. In this case, Canada would excise "Laurentia" (or "The People's Republic of Lévesquiana" as Professor David Kwavnick, whose hypothesis this is, called it) and what would be left in Canada would simply be the same province of Quebec, only smaller.

7

The Myth of Self-Determination

In the hearts of all French-Canadians there lies a pride in heritage and, to varying degrees, an attraction to the thought of an independent French state in North America. They consider themselves a people whether they live on a back-country farm or in a high-rise apartment on Montreal's fashionable Sherbrooke Street. They do not identify with France, although there are cultural and linguistic ties which, in recent years, have been reinforced.

Even French-Canadians outside of the Eastern Ontario-Quebec-northwestern New Brunswick[1] heartland have this French-Canadian connection, be they living in St-Boniface, Manitoba or Miami, Florida. They feel that they have a distinct identity with their unique history and culture, even to the style of their language, and they are proudly determined to see it survive and prosper.

It is equally true that the French-Canadian people think of Quebec as the heart of their homeland. There lies the potential confrontation. Others also look on Quebec as their home. There are more than one million non-Francophone Quebeckers, located primarily in central and western Montreal, the Eastern Townships, the Ottawa Valley, the Gaspé and the North Shore of the Gulf of St Lawrence.

In order to capitalize on this feeling of homeland, the separatists like to play the game of "majority". French-Canadians are a minority representing only 2.5 per cent of the North American population. They are a minority in Canada with 27 per cent of its population. They are the minority in the central and western part of Montreal, in two rural counties of Quebec, and on the North Shore of the Gulf of St Lawrence. Yet, they are the majority in the province overall. So, whenever attention turns to the prerogatives of the majority, they can only see the parameter that is favourable, that of the province of Quebec.

---

[1] The Francophones in the rest of New Brunswick are Acadians, not French-Canadians.

With the increased use of the name *Québécois* (discussed in the next chapter) came the ever more widely-held presumption that the map of Quebec was their territorial heritage. The fragility of this ultra-nationalist dream is exposed by any challenge. The separatists fear any discussion of divisibility of Quebec, even though they impudently harp on the division of Newfoundland, in the belief that Labrador can be taken away from that province and added to their dream country as well. Although there is no rational entitlement of French-Canadians to the whole of Quebec, it does nevertheless remain, in many hard-to-convince minds, their homeland.

When the right of self-determination is discussed among "Québécois" this presumption is taken for granted. When Fabien Roy,[2] the then member of the Quebec legislature for Beauce South, introduced his Bill 194, "An Act to recognize the right of the people of Quebec to self-determination", he was representing this attitude in the form of legislation.

When the Bill was introduced into the assembly in June of 1978, only co-author Shaw voted against it. Claude Dubois, *Union Nationale* member for Huntingdon and who has since joined the Liberals, chose to be absent rather than vote with his party, as did Zoel Saindon, the then member for Argenteuil, a Liberal. It was interesting to watch the Liberal caucus, including its five Anglophone members, struggling with conscience while they discussed how to vote on First Reading. The Liberals finally voted in favour, arguing that it was "only" the deposit of the Bill. It was "unnecessary" to vote No, they being unaware of the contents of the Bill. Their object was to avoid the suggestion that they were less nationalistic than the other parties in the house.

The preamble to Bill 194 states, "The people of Quebec is the possessor as a distinct people of . . . a historical continuity rooted in the territory of Quebec, over which it exercises its right of possession through its Government and the Legislature." The fourth paragraph of the Bill goes on to state that "The legitimacy of the [Quebec legislature] rests on the people of Quebec[3] and the [legislature] constitutes the sole legislative

---

[2] Now National Leader of the Social Credit Party.

[3] But the very next paragraph says " . . . Her Majesty . . . enacts"! Bill 194 eventually died with the end of the session but there is no doubt that it struck a responsive chord among French-speaking Quebeckers.

body the people of Quebec can regard as its own." The Bill goes on to suggest that the Quebec legislature can decide by itself the constitutional future of the province of Quebec and appeal to international bodies if interfered with.

The presumptions in the Bill are ludicrous, and so obviously unconstitutional, indeed probably seditious, that one tends to think that Roy, supposedly a Federalist, was introducing the Bill so as to dare the Federal cabinet to accept its responsibility and declare the Bill unconstitutional, thereby putting the myth of self-determination into its proper perspective.

For years now, and with ever-increasing boldness, successive Quebec governments have been publishing maps showing Labrador as part of Quebec. The French television network of the Federally-owned and -subsidized Canadian Broadcasting Corporation has been displaying such maps as a matter of course. Almost every publication or pamphlet put out by the Quebec government shows an outline purporting to represent the province of Quebec but including Labrador. Yet the government of Newfoundland has not seen fit to make any kind of official protest about this clearly unfriendly act by one province against its neighbour. When co-author Albert buttonholed Mr Joseph Smallwood[4] on this subject, the reaction was that since all Newfoundlanders consider the Quebec maps to be just a big joke, there was no call to take the matter up; and Quebec's claim to Labrador will never get anywhere anyway, since the matter had been settled once and for all by the decision of the Judicial Committee of the Privy Council in 1927, after a reference to which Quebec agreed, and after proceedings in which Quebec had a lawyer. Smallwood agreed that many Quebeckers take the Labrador claim quite seriously, but he seemed unwilling to draw the appropriate conclusion.

Here lies the crux of Canada's problem. We continue to patronize clearly unreasonable and irrational actions by Quebec ultra-nationalists rather than confront them, thereby lending credibility to their actions. Quebec is not a nation-state. It is a province, like Ontario, Manitoba and all the rest. Quebeckers are not a distinct people; they are a pluralistic society, the same as the Ontarians, the Manitobans, and all the rest.

---

[4] First Premier of Newfoundland when it became a province of Canada, and Canada's only living Father of Confederation.

L'ÉTAT ET LES COMMUNAUTÉS CULTURELLES:
Pour une action concertée

RAPPORT ET RECOMMANDATIONS
du colloque de Montréal
3 et 4 novembre 1979

Gouvernement
du Quebec

Typical Quebec Government ''Map'' Annexing Labrador, 1979

French-Canadians are a distinct people and there is a French-Canadian majority in an important part of Quebec. If they, along with the French-Canadians in such very French counties as Prescott and Russell, Ontario, and Madawaska, New Brunswick, choose, as a people, to separate themselves from Canada, provision could be made by Canada to relinquish the territory to which they are entitled. If they choose, they could appeal to international bodies as to whether the territory relinquished by Canada has been delineated with justice and equity. Of course, the Canadian government, with the support of the provincial governments of Ontario and New Brunwick and the non-Francophone minorities in central and western Montreal, the Ottawa Valley, the region south of the St Lawrence and the Gulf North Shore would also have the right to make their own case before such international bodies.

If the "debate" took these factors into account it would be rational, but when, as in the presumptions represented by Bill 194, the option is mythical, it is dangerous.

We want to put these matters into perspective. No serious person in Canada wishes to deny the French-Canadian people the right to establish their own state, if they feel that this is the solution to their problem of insecurity of language and culture. What cannot be accepted is the supposition that the prize of this decision would be the map of Quebec. This presumption can only provoke others in Quebec to claim a parallel right to self-determination.

That the map of Quebec is the prize of a "Yes" referendum result, or of any other gesture towards self-determination, is one of the illusions that Quebec ultra-nationalists, so powerful in the schools and in the media, have implanted among the population. One of the few Quebec politicians to touch even obliquely on this sore point is Claude Ryan, Leader of the Liberal Party of Quebec, who said that among the implications of Quebec leaving Canada are:

> 1) the abandonment of our share of the rights to the territory and natural resources of the rest of the country, especially the definitive and irrevocable renunciation of our fair share of the immense natural resources of the Canadian North;

2) the freezing of Quebec's territory within it present constricted boundaries, which would *at best* be those of today.[5]

It should have long since been explained that the prize was not there. Had this been done, the separatist movement would be much less of a threat. But it is a threat, even though its ultimate weapon is a dud. The result is an increasing reaction in the rest of Canada, with growing polarization and inevitably negative and reactionary attitudes. It is important that the myth of self-determination for a province be destroyed.

---

[5] *Choose Quebec AND Canada,* Liberal Party of Quebec, p. 80 (Fr. ed.) (Our italics — W.F.S. & L.A.)

8

"Québécois" — a Case of Semantic Fraud

In bygone times, before the world was fully explored, myths about strange tribes living in remote and savage places would sometimes arise. Scholars are now able to trace the origins of such myths to obscure peoples or tribes that really did exist, though distorted in the popular mind.

Here in Canada we too have a mythical people, but the myth is not religious or "folk". It is an up-to-date, 20th-century myth. As with all myths, there are some facts.

The myth is that there is a *québécois* (Quebec) people or nation. The reality, buried underneath the myth, is that there is a French-Canadian people or nation.

The noun *Québécois* simply means an inhabitant of Quebec City, just as *Montréalais* means an inhabitant of Montreal. These are the normal meanings that have existed since the 17th century. Yet, quite suddenly, after 1960, some French-Canadian ultra-nationalists began to use the word *Québécois* in place of *Canadien* (in full: *Canadien-français*) which for three centuries has meant anyone born in New France, or descended from those born in New France.

What's in a name? Much. Basically separatism faces two difficult problems: First of all, the French-Canadian people have always thought of themselves as inhabitants of Canada. In particular, the heavy movement of French out of Quebec into eastern and northern Ontario and into northern New Brunswick that has taken place over the past 125 years was never thought of as any kind of "emigration" or "exile",[1] but merely a change of province, and very much akin to the way in which hundreds of thousands of English-speaking Canadians, also over the past 125 years, have regarded a move into Quebec. In

---

[1] Unlike the emigration to the U.S.A. which gave rise to the sad folk-song *Un Canadien errant* (The Wandering [French-] Canadian).

the one case, the French in North Bay, Ontario, or Edmunston, New Brunswick, brought with them their churches and ancillary parish organizations; in the parallel case, the English in Beaconsfield, Quebec, brought with them their Rotary Clubs, Y.M.C.A.s and the other paraphenalia of Anglo-Canadian life.

And of course, there is the free flow in the other direction. The statistics of gross migration between Quebec and its two neighbouring provinces, in both directions, are quite impressive.[2] There are probably very few French Quebec families that have no near members in Ontario or New Brunswick.

In the past, French-Canadian nationalists, to the extent that they thought of separation, pictured a new country such as "Laurentia" or "Canada" (leaving the English to find another name for the remainder) that would take parts, or all, of Quebec, plus parts of Ontario and New Brunswick. The fusion of the idea of separation with the ambitions of Quebec provincial government officials and politicians to expand the limits of their power meant that the vision of the independent state had to be altered. Before this altered vision could be "sold" to the French-Canadian people, their casual attitude to residence in Ontario or New Brunswick had to be changed, using all the instruments of modern propaganda. This was a major task, for the French-Canadians are much more deep-rooted in the land called Canada than are most English-speaking Canadians who, as one witness before the Bilingualism and Biculturalism Commission said, can change their country as easily as they change an overcoat, by moving, say, to Australia or the United States. We sometimes forget that the National Anthem *O Canada!*, composed by Calixa Lavallée in 1880, was originally intended as a hymn in honour of St John the Baptist, patron saint of French Canada.

Separatists measure the degree of their penetration of the public consciousness by the extent to which the people are willing to call themselves *Québécois*. The more they can persuade the French-Canadians in Quebec to call themselves

---

[2] For example, between 1966 and 1976, 238,000 people moved from Ontario to Quebec and 382,000 from Quebec to Ontario. While the latter figure includes what one wag has called "The Station Wagon People" (English-speaking Quebeckers fleeing francization), the bulk of the numbers must represent French-Canadians.

Québécois, the easier the task of insinuating the idea that those French-Canadians who happen to live in eastern or northern Ontario or in northern New Brunswick are somehow "different" from those living in Quebec. Once that idea has been established, then the idea that Quebec's borders, which are criss-crossed daily by tens of thousands of French-Canadians, could somehow be thought of, not as casual signposts along the highway, but as a full-fledged international boundary,[3] can also be established.

It is a curious sidelight on Canadian attitudes that French-Canadians understand this point, while even quite knowledgable English-Canadians tend to say "Who cares what name they use?" An exception is James Iain Gow, Professor of Public Administration at the French-language University of Montreal, who says that the French Quebeckers "are not the only citizens of Quebec and do not represent all of French Canada. Here we see the importance of the strategy of many Quebec nationalists over the past 20 years of replacing the old title of *Canadien* by *Québécois*, and using the language of the *state of Quebec* rather than the less exalted vocabulary of *province, premier*, and so on."[4]

But there is a second reason for *Québécois*. Every survey, and all other evidence, as well as the writings of separatists of every shade, agree that only a tiny minority of separatists believe that French-Canadian sovereignty can or should be attained as the result of armed struggle.

In order to make independence look feasible it is necessary to offer some other method of attaining separation that would be convincing. Instead of armed force the path offered is moral force. The moral force that is offered to the French-Canadians is not so much the ability to sway the views of English Canada as to "shame" English Canada before the bar of a vague "international public opinion". To convince the French-Canadian voter that such a propaganda victory is within the realm of possibility, it is advantageous that as clear as possible a "case"

---

[3] This is one of the stickiest points in the P.Q. programme. Every effort is made to suggest that the boundary would be practically as open as it is now. That, and not economic worries, may be the main reason for the promise of "association".

[4] *REPORT* magazine, March, 1980.

be exhibited to the French-speaking people of Quebec to illustrate what will ultimately be presented to the world. In that
context, it is one thing to accuse English Canada of refusing to
give the French-Canadians independence; after all, what then is
"world opinion" being asked to decide? But it is quite another
to cry loud and clear QUEBEC FOR THE QUEBECKERS!
How dare English Canada, or as the same story would have it,
just plain "Canada", continue its "foreign occupation" of
"Quebec" and subjugation of the "Quebec" people! The idea
of arousing the sympathy of the outside world has a deep
appeal to the French-Canadian people and is intimately linked
to the famous "Inferiority Complex". It is by no means far-
fetched to compare the French-Canadians, who were orphaned
by France in 1763, to the orphan girl who dreams that some
day her real father will appear and turn out to be rich, aristo-
cratic and all-powerful.

When newly-elected Premier René Lévesque went to New
York to address the Economic Club, one French-Canadian, not
known to be a separatist, said to us "You've got to admit he's
got guts!"; hardly the sort of thing that anyone would say, for
example, in Halifax if Nova Scotia's Premier Buchanan were to
speak to the same group. Indeed, many observers have
remarked that Lévesque's speech irritated his listeners and lost
Quebec potential friends in Wall Street, but that the whole
speech was intended to impress the home audience.

Yet, there is a perverse desire to win the sympathy of
American opinion. René Lévesque, for example, sees the
United States as a potential friend of Quebec separatism. We
say "perverse" because the birth of the United States began
with Wolfe's conquest of Quebec, removing the hated and
feared "French menace" so that the American colonists could
start playing revolution. It continued with the direct criticism of
those provisions of the Quebec Act that preserved the French-
Canadians' religion, civil laws, and system of land tenure,
which Jefferson wrote into the Declaration of Independence
("For abolishing the free System of English Laws in a neigh-
boring Province, establishing therein an Arbitrary government,
and enlarging its Boundaries so as to render it at once an
example and fit instrument for introducing the same absolute
rule into these Colonies"), and ended in modern times with
the annihilation of the French language and culture among

three million French-Canadians in the United States.

But there is more to this business of a name. It is rich with the pseudo-problem of who is, and who is not, a Quebecker — *un Québécois*. The myth of the *Québécois* is important because it helps sustain the myth of self-determination of a province. The use of the word *Québécois* is part of that wish to will a province into a people. But self-determination is not for provinces, it is for peoples.

The name *Québécois* also belongs to millions of Quebeckers who consider themselves *Canadiens* or Canadians first, but nevertheless proud *Québécois* or Quebeckers, often with roots of many generations in their province. With the *Parti Québécois* bruiting the word *Québécois* about to denote a nationality or a future citizenship, those proud *Québécois* who are happy in their loyalty to Canada feel deprived of what for many is their birthright. A political party has stolen their name.

How did this travesty come about?

Under pressure from ultra-nationalist teachers, television "personalities" and politicians, more and more young French-Canadians began calling themselves *Québécois* instead of *Canadiens*. Part of the English-language media are following suit. At the present rate the word *Canadien*, apart from government ministry titles and the like, will survive only in the name of the famous hockey team![5] Some ultra-nationalists have even twisted the word into *Canadian* with a third "a", as in English, in order to intimidate people who wish to use the correct name, but who fear being labelled "bootlickers of the English" or *vendus* ("sold-outs").

The next step has been to distort history in order to give the impression that the French-Canadians have always been the *Québécois*. It has proved to be an effective denial of history: "You have never been called *Canadien*." Say it often enough, and . . . . For example, the historical part of the *Parti Québécois* book *L'Option* continually refers to the French-Canadians as *Québécois* and the English-speaking Canadians as *Canadiens*

---

[5] Nevertheless, a 1979 C.B.C. poll states that although 36 per cent of French Quebeckers call themselves *Québécois*, 43 per cent call themselves *Canadiens-français* and an additional nine per cent call themselves simply *Canadiens*.

(the "e" has come full circle). A typical example from *L'Option* is the description of the situation following the rebellion of 1837-38: "For the *Québécois*, the uprising was a setback, both psychologically and politically. Discouraged and humiliated by this defeat, frightened by the brutal repression by the British and the *Canadiens*, some came to reproach themselves for having believed in freedom."[6]

The terms are deliberately twisted. In the 1830s, *Canadiens* meant French-Canadians. In fact, nowhere in *L'Option* (which otherwise is liberally sprinkled with quotations) is there a quotation from any historian, or historical source, referring to the people who are supposed to be the subject of the book, by name. Apparently the *Parti Québécois* does not feel secure about the legitimacy of the name *Québécois*. It is well they do not. This omission should alert the observer to the dangerous direction in which the ultra-nationalists are moving — the falsification of history.

What is the real origin of the province's name, "Quebec"?

Before the Conquest, the colony was called New France, or Canada. "Quebec" was the name of the town.[7] And only that. On many occasions prior to the Seven Years' War, the English tried to conquer Canada by capturing the city of Quebec; succeeding only once, in 1629, when the marauding Kirke brothers from England occupied the colony until, in 1632, France regained Canada by the Treaty of St-Germain-en-Laye. The rest of Canada, such as Montreal, was an easy prize. The problem was how to take the fortress-city, protected as it was by its cliffs.

In 1759, King George II of England was in the last year of his life, but though he had a tendency to lapse into German when excited, he was keen to advance England's interests. General James Wolfe was well aware that Royalty was watch-

---

[6] p.84 (Fr. ed.)

[7] There were three administrative districts named Québec, Trois-Rivières, and Montréal but they had no significance outside of officialdom. The origin of the name "Quebec" is obscure. A popular theory is that it is an Indian word meaning "a narrowing of the river".

ing his progress, hungry for victory. And victory is what the King got.

The news of Wolfe's success on the Plains of Abraham outside the gates of Quebec struck the English world with electrifying force. In London, the despatch was made public on October 17, 1759.

"On the receipt of the foregoing news, the guns at the Park and Tower were fired, in the evening were great illuminations, bonfires, &c. in the city and sub-urbs, and the rejoicings soon after were general in all parts of the united kingdoms and Ireland . . . . His majesty was pleased to order a gratuity of 500£ to Sir James Douglas, captain of the Alcide man of war; as also to colonel Hale, who brought the account of the taking of Quebec."[8]

In all of the celebrations the word QUEBEC was the centre-piece, so much so that it began to take on an almost mystical aura. The prominent type used for the word in the fragments of poems and the reproduction of an illuminated set of windows give some idea of the emotion evoked by the name.

In the following year, 1760, George II died, and was succeeded by his grandson, George III. The coronation was a magnificent spectacle and, again, the word QUEBEC was used frequently, almost as if the town had been captured as a special gift for the coronation. London got a "Quebec Street" and generations of English schoolchildren have learnt all the details of the battle. Even today, in English radio usage, the letter "Q" is defined by the word "Quebec". The excitement was no less in the American colonies although, in keeping with their local traditions, Boston and the other New England towns turned to their preachers to set the tone of celebration. The victory of Quebec inspired a minister in New London, Connect-icut, to proclaim, "This was the Lord's doing and it is mar-vellous in our eyes!"

In the 18th century there were, of course, no electronic means of mass communication. News took time to percolate through the consciousness of the people and to be savoured

---

[8] *The MONTHLY CHRONOLOGER*, London, October, 1759.

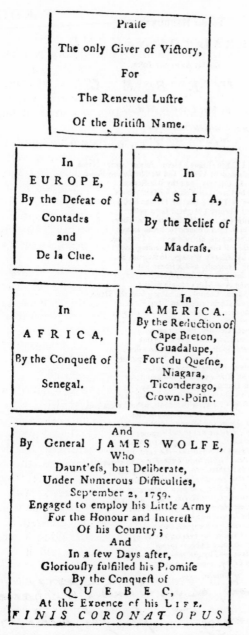

Praise

The only Giver of Victory,

For

The Renewed Luftre

Of the Britifh Name.

In
E U R O P E,
By the Defeat of
Contades
and
De la Clue.

In
A S I A,
By the Relief of
Madrafs.

In
A F R I C A,
By the Conqueft of
Senegal.

In
A M E R I C A.
By the Reduction of
Cape Breton,
Guadalupe,
Fort du Quefne,
Niagara,
Ticonderago,
Crown-Point.

And
By General J A M E S W O L F E,
Who
Daunt'efs, but Deliberate,
Under Numerous Difficulties,
September 2, 1759.
Engaged to employ his Little Army
For the Honour and Intereft
Of his Country;
And
In a few Days after,
Glorioufly fulfilled his Promife
By the Conqueft of
Q U E B E C,
At the Expence of his L I F E.
F I N I S C O R O N A T O P U S

Six Windows Much Remarked on in London, 1759

To the HONOURABLE

GENERAL *TOWNSHEND*,

On his ARRIVAL from

QUEBEC.

By Mr. *LOCKMAN.*

Obligatum redde Jovi dapem ;
Longáque feſſum Militiâ latus
Depone. HORAT. Od. 7, Lib. II.

THRICE welcome! Hero! Patriot! every Name
That's dear to Virtue, and well known to Fame.
Thy King, thy Country, hail thy ſafe Return,
Whilſt fir'd by, thee, our Youth for Glory burn.
 Tho' born to Titles ; tho' by Hymen bleſt ;
Tho' of kind Fortune's brighteſt Gifts poſſeſt :
Yet thou, with Joy, cou'dſt Honour's Call obey,
And, from each fond Connexion, break away :
Quit Pleaſures, which oft rule without Controul,
So ſtrong's their Influence o'er the yielding Soul :
And, urg'd by *Albion*'s Wrongs, to Regions fly,
Deform'd by Tempeſts, and a frozen Sky ;
To combat Savages, a hideous Race !
Whoſe ſcalping Arts Man's Origin debaſe.
 Rous'd by dread Cannon, thund'ring from the Deep,
America's great Genius roſe from Sleep :
Bid *Wolfe* advance : Immortal Wreathes obtain ;
When ſoon he fell : —O ! too untimely ſlain : —
If dying for our Country, merits Fame,
Britannia's lateſt Sons ſhall love his Name.
 Thy kindred Spirit, when his upwards flew, .
(O *Townſhend !*) did the glorious PLAN purſue.
Headed by thee, relying on thy Heart,
What generous *Briton* cou'd at Dangers ſtart ?
Not the dark Horrors of the rocky Way ;
Not ambuſh'd Indians, cou'd their Souls diſmay.
Tow'rds Victory's Fane, with Shouts, behold them riſe,
Till, o'er *Quebec*, *Britannia*'s Standard flies.
 Nor cou'd *Quebec* thy Scene triumphant cloſe ;
Thy Country's Welfare ſtill forbid Repoſe :
For told that *Conflans,* venturing on the Main,
Vow'd to diſpute, with *Hawke,* the naval Reign ;
(Hawke, a new *Ruſſell,* form'd the *French* to chace ;
Their Coaſts to frighten, and their Flag diſgrace :)
Thou, and brave *Saunders,* turning from the Shore,
Cried—" Seek the Foe, and fiery Vengeance pour."—
For ſuch RESOLVES, the *Greeks* bid Altars blaze,
And hence their Heroes gain'd eternal Praiſe.
 Flouriſh the Lawrel which adorns thy Brow ;
A Nation's Council will engroſs thee now :
For Minds like thine, for ever on the Wing,
With Ecſtacy to noble Labours ſpring.
Reſume thy Seat :—Thy gen'rous Cares renew ;
And, born to Glory, ſhine in every View.

1ſt December, 1759.

To the reverend, & very learned Dr Macro;
London 28 Dber 1759. from the Author.

An Unrecorded Poem on the Capture of Quebec, 1759

A Monumental Inscription.

Now thought worthy of a Command in Chief;
QUEBEC,
The Capital of the *French* Empire in *North America*,
Is made the Object of the important Conquest,
Expected from his great Abilities.

Art had confpired with Nature
To render the Place impregnable :
But he, undaunted amidft fuch a Scene of Difficulties,
Climbs over Rocks and Precipices,
Lays the Lower Town in Afhes,
Draws out the numerous Force of CANADA againft him,
And with lefs than five thoufand Men,
But ftout, vigorous, and ardent for Battle,
Routs and defeats them with great Slaughter.

VICTORY, alas !
Had fcarce dawned upon him with triumphant Rays of Light,
Ready to falute him,
The CONQUEROR of CANADA,
When he fell glorioufly,
Covered with honourable Wounds.

BRITONS ! rejoice and mourn :
Rejoice that your Arms have profpered
Under the Conduct of fo great a General ;
But mourn for the Lofs
Of fo good a Man,
Whofe Morals, a Copy of Gofpel-Purity,
Taught him to die contented for his Country.

To perpetuate his Memory,
This Monument was erected by the fpecial Command
Of the BRITISH SENATE and PEOPLE.
In the Year of our Lord,
One Thoufand, Seven Hundred, and Sixty.

Proposed Inscription for Monument to General Wolfe, 1760

and discussed. Not for them the television panel discussion and the instant book. Every soldier returning from the war had his own story to tell. Thus the glamour surrounding the word QUEBEC remained in the English consciousness and came to play a role a few years after Wolfe's victory, when the Seven Years' War was over and a new British province needed a name.

In the summer of 1763, the clerks and bureaucrats of Whitehall laboured, and on July 14 produced a draft letter which Lord Egremont sent to the Board of Trade for comment, stating "That the King approves the Erecting of Three New Governments in North America, under the Denominations your Lordships propose, of Canada, East Florida[9] and West Florida[10] . . ."

So the land that the French had called "Canada" was, at first, to keep its name. It included all of the territory that was described by Vaudreuil, the last French Governor, at the capitulation of Montreal, including the Ohio Valley and most of the eastern side of the Mississippi Valley. Of course, much of the territory described by Vaudreuil had previously been claimed by the English anyway. That, after all, was what the war had been about.

Apparently summer holidays were not common in those days because, with a speed that would be envied by an Ottawa bureaucrat, the Board of Trade produced its reply on August 5. They proposed that the new province of Canada comprise only the St Lawrence Valley, and that the remaining territory be under the direct control of the military, designated as a kind of reserve for the native Indians.[11] This proposal put the bureaucratic ball back in the cabinet's court, and it is there that Canada lost its name. On September 19, 1763, Lord Halifax replied to the Board of Trade on behalf of the cabinet, accepting the proposed new western boundary, in effect a straight line from Lake Nipissing to the site of the present Cornwall, adding the words:

---

[9] Now the state of Florida.

[10] Now the coastal parts of the states of Alabama and Mississippi.

[11] This caused problems because there were French settlements at Vincennes (now in Indiana) and elsewhere. Eventually, the settlers were allowed to stay where they were.

The New Provinces and the "Indian Territory", 1763

That such Government be described in the Commission, as comprehending all such Part of Canada on the North Side of the River St. Laurence, and all such Parts of His Majesty's antient Colonies of Nova Scotia, New England, and New York, on the South Side of the said River, as lie within the Limits above mentioned, and that It be called the Province of Quebec.

Apparently the First Recorded Use of the Name Province of Quebec. Lord Halifax to the Board of Trade, September 19, 1763

"That such Government . . . be called the Province of Quebec."

This was apparently the first recorded use of the new name — Quebec as a province. It seems probable that the Whitehall officials were decisively influenced in their choice of name by the ever-present ripples of excitement over Wolfe's victory. The September 19 letter was the basis of the Royal Proclamation, and also of General Murray's commission as first Governor. It set the seal on the British Conquest and, by cutting off direct access to the "Indian Territory", made clear for the first time to the French-Canadian people that they were indeed a conquered people. The document affirmed that they could, at best, hope only to share, as one British colony among many, the fur trade of the interior, instead of having it all to themselves, as before. (It tells us something about our own time that history can be so twisted by self-seeking politicians that hundreds of thousands of the descendants of the French colonists who were aggrieved by the conqueror's bureaucratic decision on the western boundary of their homeland, giving it the name "Province of Quebec", now proudly support a "Quebec Party" and place stickers on their cars reading, "I have a yen for Quebec".)

The word "Quebec" as the name of the province remained in official use,[12] under the terms of the Quebec Act, until 1791. Then, perhaps in deference to the feelings of the French-Canadians,[13] who considered themselves *Canadiens*, and the

---

[12] But "Canada" was the preferred name even among English officials.

[13] In signing the message to Parliament urging passage of the bill, the King wrote, "I have signed the Messages to the two Houses of Parliament respecting the Province of Quebec, and shall be happy if the alterations proposed prove agreeable to the different classes of subjects in that Province, but must ever think that those who have the strongest claim on the attention of this country are the old inhabitants, whose rights and usages ought by no means to be disturbed." — Letter of February 24, 1791 in the Fortescue MSS.— *The Later Correspondence of George III*, Vol. I, p. 519. The "alterations" refer to the fact that what we call the Constitutional Act or Canada Act was piloted through Parliament as a series of amendments to the Quebec Act. — In his letter of October 20, 1789 to Dorchester, Secretary of State William Grenville said " . . . a considerable degree of attention is due to the prejudices and habits of the French inhabitants . . ." (The word "prejudice" did not then carry the pejorative connotation that it does now.)

excitement over Wolfe's victory having died down, the two halves of what was now being called a "country" were named "Upper Canada" and "Lower Canada".

The name "Quebec", for anything except the city, fell out of use for the next 76 years. Officially, the inhabitants were "Upper-Canadians" and "Lower-Canadians". In practice, the French called themselves *Canadiens* as they always had, or, when discussing political matters, *Bas-Canadiens* (Lower-Canadians).

In 1841, the two provinces were combined under the name "Canada".

Early in 1867, the Fathers of Confederation had not yet agreed on names for the two new provinces to be created using the halves of the province of Canada, being accustomed to referring to them as Upper Canada and Lower Canada (although officially supposed to be called, under the Act of Union, "Canada West" and "Canada East"). Since the name "Canada" had been chosen for the whole of the new country from coast to coast, the names "Upper Canada" and "Lower Canada" were thought to be inappropriate.[14] As a solution, Colonial Office officials in London suggested that "Quebec" once more serve duty as the name of the lower, easternmost, half. And that is how the present province of Quebec was named.

And that is how the present province of Ontario was named! Although it had been over a century since Wolfe's victory, the Colonial Office was well aware that it was the name of the city of Quebec that was their source for the proposed name of the lower province. For that reason it seemed logical to name the upper half of the former province of Canada "Toronto" and, *mirabile dictu*, that is exactly what they did![15]

---

[14] A rather small-minded attitude. The two provinces in the heart of Holland are called "North Holland" and "South Holland", even though that country has nine other provinces.

[15] The English had established a precedent for giving a colony the same name as its chief town when they took over the Dutch colony in the Hudson River valley. The Dutch had called the chief town "New Amsterdam" and the colony as a whole "New Netherlands" or "New Belgium", the latter name being favoured because most of the promoters of the colony were Protestant Belgians who had fled Antwerp and taken up residence in Amsterdam. (It was the movement of the Belgian Protestants

The delegates from Canada, in London at the time, must have balked at the choice, so the British officials, upon learning that Toronto was situated on a lake, enquired the lake's name and dubbed the new province "Ontario" instead. After that brilliant feat, the Whitehall bureaucrats must have felt that they had done a good day's work and gone out and treated themselves to a brandy-and-soda.

While officials in London thought "Quebec" quite suitable as the name of the new lower province, ordinary folk found it hard to get used to. For years, mail had been addressed to "Montreal, Lower Canada" or "Montreal, Canada East", or simply, "Montreal, Canada". People felt stupid writing "Montreal, Quebec", just as they would now if they had to write "Hamilton, Toronto" or "Calgary, Edmonton". The habit naturally arose of writing Montreal, "Province of Quebec", which evolved through "P. Quebec" and "P. Que." to the present-day "P.Q.".[16] As the years passed, the province grew in importance and the city of Quebec declined. In later years "Quebec" has come to mean the province more than the city — hence the need for the modern term "Quebec City".[17]

The flurry of new names did not faze the French-Canadians. They went on calling themselves *Canadiens* although the new name of the province confused them as much as anyone else. In France, a city and a province may have roughly similar

to Holland that turned Amsterdam into one of Europe's leading commercial centres, which it still is, and its then larger rival, Antwerp, into a second-rate town, which it still is, three hundred years later. The parallel with Toronto and Montreal today is painfully reminiscent.) — When the English took over the Dutch colony, King Charles II wished to rename it in honour of his younger brother, James, Duke of York. Hence, the name "New York". This was in keeping with the old English practice of giving a city and a county the same name, e.g. Nottingham, Derby, Durham, Worcester, or Huntingdon. The last-named is repeated in the county and village of that name in Quebec.

16 The separatists naturally detest this use of "P.Q.", as they refuse to accept the meaning of the "P" (province).

17 The French have no such problem as the distinction is automatically looked after by rules of grammar. *A Québec* means in or to Quebec City. *Au Québec* (literally "to the Quebec") means in or to Quebec province. The English usage is parallel to the term "New York City" which is frequently used in the northeast of the U.S. to distinguish the city from the state.

names but not the very same name, examples being Tours in Touraine, Poitiers in Poitou, or Angers in Anjou. It may be that the more nationalistic did not like the new name of the province because of its association with the Conquest, although we have no direct evidence of this. A. A. Dorion's anti-Confederation newspaper *Le Pays* did not comment at length on the new name. However, in its issue of February 23, 1867, under the headline STUPIDITY, it reported:

" . . . . the name of Upper Canada will be 'Toronto' and the name of Lower Canada, 'Quebec'." By February 26, the names "Ontario" and "Quebec" were known to be definite and *Le Pays* said "Lower Canada will be called Province of Quebec. Today we say, when speaking of the former capital, Quebec (Lower Canada); in the future we shall say Quebec (Quebec) or, going even further, Montreal (Quebec). How cute!"

The pro-Confederation *La Minerve* was effusive in its praise of the new name. Its London "editorial correspondent" suggested that the people of the new province would henceforth be called "Québécquois, as our forefathers were called for a very long time", a phrase as mendacious as the fake antique spelling of *Québécois*. Sir George-Étienne Cartier, a Father of Confederation, and owner of *La Minerve*, was nothing if not a super-salesman of the project. But his place in history is apparently not so secure. Some ultra-nationalists have called him *le premier des lâcheurs* (the first of the tricksters) — and this example of foisting the fake name "Québécquois" on the public gives the insult a grain of truth. But what of today's political super-salesmen? The very people who called Cartier a trickster are up to the same 110-year-old trick themselves!

Still, honest distaste for the name "Quebec" for the province continues to our own day. For example, in the 1950s Raymond Barbeau, a leading separatist, wrote:

" 'Quebec', as such, is, to put it bluntly, insipid and insignificant. The term is irremediably attached to the *province* that was created in 1764 (sic), *after the conquest* . . . 'Quebec' must disappear at the same time as the shield surmounted by the Imperial crown of England . . . " [18]

---

[18] *La Laurentie*, no. 101, pp. 23-24. Referring to the present official coat of

The Quebec Coat of Arms: Art Lobel, Curler

La Revue indépendantiste states, "The English reduced our territory to a small reservation along the river. The name Quebec is thus linked to a terrible humiliation inflicted on our ancestors."[19] Earlier separatists preferred to name the proposed independent French-speaking country "Laurentia" (after the St Lawrence River), a name which they used before the 1960s. Apart from the dislike for the name "Quebec", the use of "Laurentia" helped avoid the problem of boundaries. Some separatists wished Laurentia to include large parts of Ontario, all of New Brunswick, and part of New England, along with most or all of Quebec.

To advance their cause the separatists promoted an "Estates-General of French Canada", a gathering of representatives of all French-Canadians and Acadians. This gambit was not a success. It proved an exercise in frustration to think in terms of French-Canadian independence. But a solution was in sight. In the early 1960s, the separatists saw their chance at harnessing to their ideas the power-hunger of the provincial government and of the rising generation of ambitious young politicians. Hence, the sudden affection for the name "Quebec" and the mythical *québécois* people. Hence, finally, the *Parti Québécois*.

The flavour of the relationship between sincere separatists and the slick, professional politicians of the *Parti Québécois* is well expressed in *La Revue indépendantiste*, " . . . it is unfortunate that some people are trying to make us abandon our glorious name CANADIENS to be replaced by the evil-sounding sobriquet *Québécois*. The *Canadiens* are us. We should not allow anyone else to steal that name from us. Freeing ourselves from colonialism includes that. We hope that some day someone will request M. René Lévesque (who was opposed to the name *Québécois* for his party) to arrange that we keep our traditional name of *canadien* people when the independent republic, which we all desire, is proclaimed. The English in the other provinces will adopt whatever name they like for the

---

arms of the Province of Quebec which includes British symbols. This emblem has fallen into obscurity, although occasionally used by Anglo-Quebec sports organizations.

[19] Summer, 1978, p. 26.

country that will remain to them. They have absolutely no right to take from us the name by which we have always been known. Moreover, no one has the right to abandon it."[20] Even the provincial Civil Service sometimes balks at the name "Quebec". The provincial library service refers to what one would expect to be called "Quebeciana" (miscellaneous classification relating to Quebec) as *Laurentiana*. So "Laurentia" has not died.

By calling themselves *Parti Québécois*, by first encouraging, and then intimidating the French-Canadian people into calling themselves *Québécois*, so that even the traditional pea soup has to be called an example of *québécois* cookery, the ultra-nationalists hope to hide the cracks in their specious claim to the whole territory of the province. The same tactic is designed to justify turning the provincial government (a creation of the British North America Act and constitutionally established to administer, at the junior level, the territory of Quebec, providing services to its residents regardless of language) into an exclusive instrument of and for their own aggrandizement. That is also the significance of the change of name of the provincial Legislative Assembly to that of *Assemblée Nationale* (National Assembly). The whole affair is a kind of semantic fraud.

American readers might picture the situation if the Mexican-American population in California happened to be the majority in that state and some unscrupulous political leaders demanded that California be separated from the United States. They would start by suddenly dropping the name "Mexican-American" or "Chicano" and begin to call themselves "Californians" instead — even to the point of writing new history books implying that the Mexican-Americans within California have "always" been called *Californians*.

What is remarkable to the point of astonishment is that a large number of French-Canadians have willingly adopted the name *Québécois*, knowing, from their history, that the name "Quebec" is a badge of the Conquest. It is doubly remarkable and astonishing that in adopting the name *Québécois*, a shabby, modern, "ad-agency" name concocted in the early 1960s, they are rejecting the time-honoured term *Canadien* which they had

[20] Summer, 1978, p. 58.

proudly used for over three centuries. Lord Durham was wrong when he called the French-Canadians 'a people without a history'. Yet the *Parti Québécois* seems to be intent on proving him right!

There is a kind of mass collective falsehood, with every French-Canadian under pressure to call himself *Québécois*. An illustration of this occurred in 1977 during a visit by Premier René Lévesque to St-Georges-de-Beauce. An elderly gentleman was pleased by the Premier's remarks and got up to tell him so. The gentleman went on to say that in his opinion Lévesque was a good *Canadien*. There was an embarassed silence, followed by nervous laughter. The old man had not learnt his lines!

This shabby tactic of inviting a whole people to join in a fraud was reflected in the official slogan of the "Yes" committee for the 1980 referendum, *Au Québec — on sait ce qu'on veut* ("In Quebec — we know what we want"), with its unmistakable connotation of hoodwinking English Canada. ("We" know what we want but "They" don't.) This tactic is so transparent to French-Canadians that striking public service employees, probably separatist to a man, deliberately sang *O Canada!* at a demonstration in front of the provincial legislative building. It was their way of "needling" the *Parti Québécois* cabinet ministers; of saying, "We all know what you're up to and don't think the same weapon can't be used against you!"[21]

What can make a proud people behave like a troupe of mountebanks, acting out a script in order to impress the Anglophones in the audience? The answer to this question lies in a kind of illness that has preyed on the collective character of the French-Canadians for some 200 years. It is an illness which will soon have run its course, but which is now in that last state of fever which signals the onset of the crisis that must come before the patient gets well.

---

[21] While we find ourselves in sharp disagreement with Claude Ryan, leader of the Quebec Liberal Party, on language law and constitutional reform, we grant that, in the manner of his leadership, he represents an alternative not just to René Lévesque but to the squalid play-acting implicit in the *Parti Québécois* approach. To the extent that the French of Quebec consciously transfer their partisan allegiance from Lévesque to Ryan, they will unconsciously be making a statement in favour of a kind of dignity.

9

The "Inferiority Complex"

The reason why many French-Canadians, perhaps the majority, are willing to support collectively a role that is often at variance with reality is that they are convinced that they need this kind of distortion in order to compensate for their disadvantages. So powerful and deep-rooted is this national "Inferiority Complex" that only a small minority is entirely free of it. Millions, even against their better judgment, are sufficiently affected by it to accept, if not to support, some of the wildest propositions of the ultra-nationalists.

An example is the attitude when the Prime Minister of Canada is French-Canadian. The French-Canadians are pleased when a Laurier or a St-Laurent or a Trudeau holds that high office. Among English-speaking Canadians there is little doubt that, as Prime Minister, Pierre-Elliott Trudeau is in charge; indeed probably the most powerful individual in Canadian history. Yet, French-Canadian insecurity is such that — based on the number who have made the point with us — probably nine French-Canadians out of ten are firmly convinced that Trudeau has only limited power; that there are shadowy English-speaking advisers who control him; and that an English-speaking Prime Minister has much more real power in fact.[1] This does not mean that the individual French-Canadian suffers from an inferiority complex — far from it. Few peoples exhibit so much self-confidence individually. Note the excellent expression *Pas de problème!* meaning "Don't worry, I (or we) can do it (or) obtain it (or) repair it". No, as an illness, the "Inferiority Complex" is strictly collective.

It can be said that while, like any other people, the French-Canadians have their weaknesses as well as their strengths,

---

[1] Commenting on the 1979 defeat of Trudeau: "English Canada had enough of this group of Quebeckers to whom they had given the appearance of power. They decided to take back the appearance as well as the realities of power." — René Lévesque at St-Georges-de-Beauce, *The Gazette*, August 8, 1979.

they do not now suffer from any real disadvantage. It is true that they have to learn English more often than English-speaking Canadians have to learn French. This handicap can never be removed since English is the dominant language of North America, as it is of the commercial centre of Montreal. Even this drawback has become less important in recent years. Now that five or six million French-speaking Canadians have achieved North American levels of income and education, the French-language market alone in Quebec, Ontario, and New Brunswick has become so big and elaborate that the proportion of French-Canadians who need any but the most rudimentary knowledge of English has declined. It is quite feasible, for example, for the unilingual French-Canadian to travel to Florida and receive a wide range of services in his own language. On the other hand, the "top achievers" need English as much as they ever did, perhaps even more. For example, the French-Canadian-owned National Bank of Canada is expanding in English Canada, so headquarters management must now use more English. The successful "Québecor" publishing group has launched an English-language daily newspaper in Philadelphia, thus increasing the need to use English in the Montreal head office.

On the score of language, the French-Canadians need not feel concerned about the inherent disadvantage. Many English-speaking Quebeckers can speak French and do so in the course of business, especially in sales work. That puts the French-Canadians at a great advantage over, for example, the Dutch-speaking people in Europe: 12 million in Holland and five million in Belgium. Virtually no one outside of these 17 million people speaks a word of Dutch, yet they never complain[2] about having to carry the burden of bilingualism, or, in their case, multilingualism. Certainly the Dutch harbour no inferiority complex on this account; nor do the Danes, the Norwegians, the Swedes, the Finns, the Hungarians, or any other modern people whose language is spoken by a small minority of a continent's population.

---

[2] There is resentment, particularly against the Germans, who pour over the border in their hundreds of thousands in the summer and never even consider for a moment that they ought at least to try to speak something other than German. The resentment is of course due to the last war. In any case, it is rarely divulged to outsiders.

Why then this feeling of inferiority? We are convinced that the answer to this question lies in the past; we see nothing whatever in the present to justify it. The French-Canadians have everything and every opportunity and every freedom that modern life can offer, and know it. They live a better life than they would if they were still in a colony or dependency of France, and know it. They know well that the British Conquest, and the Quebec Act and subsequent British laws whose spirit is embodied in our present Confederation, have given them both the protection of their own language and customs, and the advantages of the North American economy, while preserving them from assimilation into the American melting pot where, even in border towns such as Plattsburgh, New York, almost in the suburbs of Montreal, the French language has been wiped out simply because of not being inside Canada.[3] They know that even if Wolfe had lost the Battle of the Plains of Abraham, and even if the American revolutionaries had respected the borders of New France, Napoleon would have sold the colony to the United States, along with Louisiana, in 1803.

Knowing all this, they still feel that they need every special advantage that government can give them. They are convinced that in fair and open competition they would always lose. Perhaps no one today exemplifies the "Inferiority Complex" more than Camille Laurin, the *Parti Québécois* Minister for Cultural Development, a man of dedication and intelligence. It was Dr Laurin who said, in a full-dress interview, "The State of Quebec [is] the only capitalist that we have", implying that French-Canadians lack the ability to suceed in the free market. It speaks volumes about the intellectual atmosphere in French Quebec today that not one of the many successful French-Canadian businessmen replied to this insult. Journalist Hubert Gendron, commenting on Dr Laurin's "extraordinary" remarks, wrote that "the interview shows that the Minister has a rather low opinion of French-speaking Quebeckers . . ."[4]

---

[3] ". . . the church built as 'Saint-Pierre' in 1891 has now become 'St. Peter's'; sermons in French were discontinued as far back as 1946." — *Languages in Conflict*, p. 72.

[4] *The Montreal Star*, March 11, 1978. Dr Laurin was interviewed by *Ici Québec* magazine, March, 1978.

Dr Laurin enrages Anglo-Quebeckers by suggesting that they shouldn't be troubled by his harsh language law — if they wish to see an English sign they can always travel to Ontario or the United States, he says. To the English this is like being told that they can be "let out of prison on a pass". To Dr Laurin the mere fact that Anglo-Quebeckers *are* English-speaking gives them a tremendous, almost mysterious, advantage, so that any complaints are mere quibbles. Even with the harsh language laws, the French-Canadian, he feels, is terribly handicapped. But when it comes to itemizing the handicaps, Dr Laurin, or indeed any French-Canadian ultra-nationalist, refuses to be pinned down or simply repeats statistics that are either distorted or simply do not pertain to anything that can fairly be called a handicap.

Statistics are brought forward to show that the average income of French-Canadians is lower than that of some other groups. The implication is that there is some sort of externally-imposed handicap. But this is never explained. We never know what the handicap is.

As in all these questions, it is not the substance of the argument but rather its purpose, to score points in political debate, that matters. That is why the earnest efforts of many English-speaking Canadians to "explain" the advantages of Confederation, to encourage contacts by visits and meetings, or to learn French, while useful and commendable, can have little bearing on French-Canadian political attitudes. Until the "Inferiority Complex" is understood, it cannot be exorcised. Until English Canada understands that by appeasing and pandering to demands for special privileges and concessions that go beyond fair treatment, it is only encouraging support for ultra-nationalism; there will be no solution; and the "Inferiority Complex" will continue to draw nourishment.

The roots of the "Inferiority Complex" lie in the history of French Canada. While the French-Canadians today are a people who can hold their heads high, who demonstrate achievement in all walks of life, and who have attained a high standard of education and income, the situation was very different as little as 20 years ago.

For the nearly 200 years from the Conquest in 1760 to the 1950s, the French-Canadians had understandable reasons for their "Inferiority Complex". The mass of the original colonists in New France, particularly the men, did not come here because of any strong wish to do so. Rather, they were cajoled and pushed. The main reason for coming was to share in the excitement and opportunities for exploration of the interior and the fur trade. " . . . in every colonist slept a Cortez whom the thirst for riches and exotic places threatened to awaken."[5] They preferred to live in the towns, where they were close to these opportunities. The clergy, too, were keen explorers, anxious to find new Indian tribes to convert.

The English colonies to the south were much more heavily populated, and that by settlers seeking religious and political freedom and the chance to make their own way, especially through individual ownership of land. The English colonies were more an end in themselves than a means of reaching China or of trading in furs. Early on, the French authorities, under Jean-Baptiste Colbert, decided that colonization would be the only way to hold on to Canada, and that this had to be sponsored. It is a facet of their national character, and still the case today, that emigration is deeply repugnant to the Frenchman. If ever told that opportunities are few in France and plentiful abroad, the Frenchman answers 'Good - let my neighbour emigrate; I will stay.' Most Frenchmen are half-convinced that anyone who has emigrated must be running away from trouble or scandal.

Under Colbert, several thousand men were gently "pushed" into going to Canada. However, this would not guarantee a permanent population. Pressure was then exerted to promote the formation of family life. In certain areas, such as Rouen, whose Bishop was a friend of the King, devout families each gave up a daughter to emigrate to Canada. These were the famous *filles du roi* (the King's girls), chosen also for their wholesome good looks which probably explains why the French-Canadians are a handsome race. Again, with direct encouragment from the King, officers and gentlemen took up grants of seigniories in New France. Local agricultural settlement gave permanence to the colony and reduced dependence on supply ships from France.

---

[5] *La Nouvelle France*, p. 79.

If the matter had been completely up to the King and Colbert, France would have had a healthier colony in Canada. Unfortunately, the people were not interested. In the last 80 years of French rule, when Colbert's ideas were out of fashion and the authorities had given up "pushing" emigration, few new colonists arrived. It is thought that about 3,500, mostly discharged soldiers, were counted as arrivals in the period 1740-60, but it is not clear how many stayed in Canada. The religious conflict within France and the expulsion of the Protestants, together with the fact that only Catholics were allowed to enter Canada, had a negative effect.

Somewhat reluctantly, the *Canadien*, encouraged not only by Governor, priest, and *seigneur*, but also by wife, took up farming, but his heart was never in it. His eye was on the goings-on in Quebec, Three Rivers, and Montreal. He was never out of touch because an excellent road was built along the St Lawrence. It was as if all Canada lived along one busy street.

Hence, it was not a placid rural society that merely "changed hands" with the Conquest. If was, rather, a population that had been "parked", not too willingly, in the countryside, yet psychologically centred on the three towns, and, through them, the exploration of, and trade with, the vast continental interior.

With the Treaty of Paris in 1763, France gave up Canada. The military, the Governor and his staff, and many of the *seigneurs* and merchants returned to the mother country. The mass of the people who stayed, other than the clergy, did so more from necessity than choice, being either too poor to move, or fearful of arriving friendless in a France from which they were separated by several generations. The respectful behaviour of the English occupation troops in the period 1760-63 was a further encouragement to stay. But there can be no doubt that all who stayed became conscious of being at a disadvantage compared to those who had left. And so, the "Inferiority Complex" began to germinate.

The first years of the English occupation were spent in fear that the French-Canadians would suffer the same fate as the Acadians, namely dispossession and exile. Fortunately, the same strategic motives that had led England to treat the Acadians harshly resulted in the liberal Quebec Act for the French-

Canadians. Yet the fear of reprisal left its mark. The three towns now seemed to offer opportunity to the English. The *Canadiens* felt constrained to stay on the seigniories, to 'keep out of the way', although when offered they eagerly took up jobs as *voyageurs* in the fur trade.

As their original presence in Canada had been at the behest of their King, specifically to advance France's interest, and since they could hardly serve this interest now that England was their master, the French-Canadians in time developed a sense of having no purpose — of being useless. As historians have observed, "For the 65,000 survivors of New France, there began henceforth not a second phase of their history but the first phase of a new history in which they would certainly be intimately involved but which, in the final analysis, could just as easily take place without them."[6]

Those haunting words give some idea of the deep emotional pull felt by separatists today — emotions that the leaders of the *Parti Québécois* turn to their own political advantage. But in the real event of 1763, and the growing realization in the years 1763 to 1789 that Canada would never again belong to France, the feeling of purposelessness must have been almost palpable, and must have reinforced the "Inferiority Complex" considerably.

By 1800, the "Inferiority Complex" was a factor, but yet to reach its zenith. The next, perhaps decisive, stage in its growth came with the arrival of English-speaking settlers in the townships and in the "English" seigniories of Lower Canada.

Many French-Canadians — perhaps a majority — had never considered agriculture their true vocation. The clergy, for some reason, often insisted that only one crop, wheat, be planted, year after year. Fertilization was unknown, except presumably to the religious orders, who apparently did not share their knowledge with the ordinary people. Manure was thrown away, to the point where piles of nature's fertilizer stood on the ice of the St Lawrence each winter, literally turning the river brown in the spring.

This was in sharp contrast to the Loyalist and Scotch and Irish settlers, whose purpose in coming to Canada was to obtain land for farming. The newcomers applied crop rotation and

---

[6] *La Nouvelle France*, p. 210.

used fertilizer. They produced excellent crops even on land that had been abandoned by French-Canadians. It was to be a long time before French-Canadians were to apply modern techniques not only to agriculture but also to dairying and horticulture,[7] both of which, in their commercial form, were introduced to Lower Canada by English-speaking settlers.

Today, the French-Canadian farmer, dairyman, or grower is as thoroughly up to date as any, but the mental scars resulting from generation after generation watching from the sidelines while the English-speaking almost "magically" produced rich crops, tons of milk, and carloads of apples, have yet to heal. These mental scars are more evident among present-day urban French-Canadians, some generations removed from the countryside. Happily, the present generation of rural French-Canadians seems to suffer relatively little from the "Inferiority Complex".

With the coming of the Industrial Revolution to Lower Canada, there was the same phenomenon of watching from the sidelines, or, later, of becoming junior, unskilled employees while the English-speaking looked after everything that required education or skill. This was very much the case during the authors' boyhood. It is only in the last 20 years that French-Canadians have begun en masse to tackle industrial jobs that require education and skill. Considering that a whole series of generations, from 1840 to 1950, found, from early childhood, that, almost invariably, the man who "took charge" of anything technical, or the man who knew how to repair a complicated machine, or the man who travelled, or the man who was rich, was English-speaking, it is not surprising that 20 years is not long enough to exorcise the "Inferiority Complex".

Up to 1950, the disparity between average incomes of French-Canadians and English-speaking Canadians was so evident that there could be no argument concerning the fact. A typical statistical contrast can be seen in average Retail Merchandise trade per capita, 1941, for some selected localities:

---

[7] As late as 1896, the great majority of the members of the Pomological and Fruit-Growing Society of the Province of Quebec were English-speaking. There was a small but keen representation of French-Canadians in these societies, but the mass were in no hurry to use the new techniques.

French Localities	English Localities
French Localities	**English Localities**
Drummondville, P.Q. . . $433	Truro, N.S. $840
Three Rivers, P.Q. $321	Kitchener, Ont. $505

Another contrast was in Gross Postal Revenue, 1943, per capita:[8]

Chicoutimi P.Q. $4.10	Brandon, Man. $7.89
Sorel, P.Q. $3.36	Kitchener, Ont. $6.54

Today the disparity is so small that Quebec government sociologists feel compelled to include doubtful sets of figures in order to prove disparities worth discussing. Any disparity that may exist now, even if it could be proved, is arguably a cause for grievance, but not, as were the wide disparities before 1950, grist to the mills of the "Inferiority Complex".

The disparity in level of education between French-Canadians and English-speaking Canadians was also very wide. Compulsory education was not introduced in Quebec until 1942. That should not be taken to mean that illiteracy was common. Neither was it a rarity. Quebec was particularly behind in the provision of public libraries:

Public Libraries, 1941

	Circulation	Registered Borrowers
Quebec[9]	729,000	24,800
Ontario	13,596,000	678,200

Today, French Quebec has many schools, colleges, and universities as well as its own flourishing publishing industry. There are busy French-language bookstores everywhere.

Health and nourishment were another area of immense disparity. Before 1950, French-Canadians had very high rates of diseases such as tuberculosis, extremely low levels of dental care and were of very low average height.

---

[8] 1941 population.

[9] Even in Quebec, the public libraries were mainly in English-speaking municipalities. This is one of the last areas being tackled by the Quiet Revolution.

No one was surprised by such statistics as these:

Children under One Year of Age
Death Rates per 1,000 Live Births

English-speaking towns:	1926-30*	1931-35*	1936-40*	1941†	1942†
Brantford, Ont.	76	54	50	53	31
Calgary, Alta	69	44	37	37	33
Kingston, Ont.	99	58	55	54	43
Windsor, Ont.	73	52	40	31	44
French-speaking towns:					
Thetford Mines, P.Q.	113	91	85	73	58
Chicoutimi, P.Q.	129	112	91	81	79
Sorel, P.Q.	187	136	129	117	85
Three Rivers, P.Q.	171	200	184	71	64

*By place of occurence   † By place of residence.

Today, the average level of health care, of nourishment,[10] and of small children's dental care in French Quebec is virtually the same as among English-speaking Canadians. The young people at Quebec's French-language schools and universities are bursting with good-looking vitality and health, and they are just about as tall as any group of Quebec Anglophones. Quebec easily swept the 1979 Canadian Winter Games, a feat of a sort that would have been unheard-of 40 years ago.

But the two centuries of inferiority are not that easily washed out of the minds of French-Canadians. This was noticed by a writer for the *National Geographic* magazine, April 1977:

"What'll happen to the Québécois? I think back on my conversations with these traditionally expansive talkers. Often what I heard, alas, came out of traditional pessimism and unhappy experience.

"For example, a country priest: 'The English have always treated us as inferior, and so we feel inferior. It's deep in our subconscious . . .'

"A housewife: 'To feel threatened is part of our heritage. Our schoolbooks were full of how the British beat us 200 years ago, that they're strong and we're weak. It's an underdog feeling. You fear you can't make it . . .'

---

[10] Montreal supermarkets have almost given up trying to sell cheap "no name" grocery products in French-speaking districts, yet they are accepted in English-speaking areas.

"A lawyer: 'My mother wouldn't buy a stove made in Quebec. She said how could it be any good? We don't trust ourselves; we're almost glad when we don't succeed . . .' "

This lack of self-confidence has provided a golden opportunity to ultra-nationalist politicians who augment their power by claiming to be able to give to the French-speaking majority that which they fear they are incapable of getting for themselves, namely the commanding positions of economic power.

Thus, French-Canadians believe that they must be given a special "edge" in order to be able to compete in Canada. In Quebec, they feel that requiring things to be done in French gives them that edge. *Il faut exiger le français au Québec* (We must require French in Quebec) is the cry. Nevertheless, they would like to see bilingualism in the rest of Canada, especially in employment, for they know that, in spite of costly programmes to teach French to Anglophones, those posts that are designated as "bilingual" are filled primarily by French-Canadians.

Thus the rationale for language legislation such as Bill 22 and Bill 101, and francization generally. The lever that they feel they must have in order to gain acceptance for this in English-speaking Canada is their threat of separation. To many Canadians, a French Quebec in a bilingual Canada is an acceptable solution. To them, the English minority in Quebec especially should accommodate, or move.

Thus we have a Quebec that is being de-anglicized, and becoming a region where things economic are done in French. The trouble is, this means those things that can be done in French are remaining, and the rest, which by preference or by necessity function in English, are leaving. This has led to the tragedy of the exodus.

10

The Tragedy of the Exodus

The vote of the policyholders of the Sun Life Assurance Company of Canada in 1978 was an example of the malaise that grips Quebec today. The leadership of the Liberal Party had gone to Claude Ryan, a proclaimed friend of the minorities. The Liberals were showing healthy gains in public opinion polls. All indicators were that they would be in a position to win the next provincial election. As well, poll after poll indicated that the *Parti Québécois* was not achieving momentum in its drive for a "Yes" vote in the proposed referendum. In spite of these signs of potential improvement in Quebec's political climate, 84 per cent of the policyholders voted to move Sun Life's head office from Montreal to Toronto.

The Sun Life executives were bold in making known their intentions of leaving the province, and frank in saying why.[1] Having been established in Montreal 110 years earlier they had every right to take much of the credit for the growth of the insurance industry in that city. In 1960, over 160 insurance companies were doing business other than sales in Montreal, and with the help of Sun Life, Montreal was not only the centre of the insurance industry in Canada, but also one of the centres of insurance world-wide. Yet, by the time Sun Life made their announcement, the number of companies had dwindled to fewer than thirty, most of the decline having occurred before the P.Q. victory but during the ultra-nationalist thrust of the 60s and early 70s.

The same phenomenon has been seen in all branches of business expertise in Montreal. The city was at one time the money and banking, including foreign exchange, centre of Canada. The trust companies were centred here as were representatives of international banks. The Montreal Stock Exchange was the major financial and industrial securities market in Canada. Montreal was the principal centre in this country for

---

[1] So intense was the criticism that the Sun Life later equivocated.

the floating of municipal, provincial and Federal government loans.

There are still a good number of head offices in Montreal, but many major functions have been transferred elsewhere, usually to Toronto. One Montreal bank is setting up a vast computer centre in a suburb of Toronto, which, counting the regional Ontario service, will ultimately employ 2,000 people. Toronto is now the centre of financial activity, with Montreal rapidly declining into a branch office operation. In the case of some smaller firms, there is only a Montreal telephone number, with a tie to the Toronto office. Some firms by-pass even this sham and show only their Toronto telephone number, or a toll-free long-distance number, in the Montreal directory. Several prestigious international and Canadian firms, and also some important companies in, for example, the computer industry, simply do not bother to maintain any presence in Montreal, even though they have branches in as many as half a dozen Canadian cities.

Between 1960 and 1965, employment in financial institutions in Montreal was still growing at a rate of 26 per cent a year, while Toronto's corresponding rate was 15 per cent. By 1977, employment in Toronto in financial houses was growing at the rate of 33 per cent a year. In Montreal it was declining.

It is often suggested that the decline of Montreal and the rise of Toronto are the result of a North American "drift" of head offices and business in general to the west. This widely-believed suggestion was demolished in an article by co-author Albert[2] who pointed out that there is no geographical advantage in moving to Toronto. There is no "natural" reason for Toronto to prosper while Montreal languishes. Toronto's industrial hinterland is not as healthy as Montreal's. The Great Lakes cities are declining as head office centres. Cleveland is one of the worst hit, and Cleveland is in many ways almost a twin to Toronto. Toronto's other neighbours, Detroit, Toledo, Buffalo and Rochester are all in decline.

In Canadian conditions, "natural" drift towards Toronto is even less credible. As French becomes ever more important as a language in the retail and employment markets it behoves firms doing business all over Canada to move *to* Montreal so

---

[2] "Westward Hokum!", *REPORT* magazine, December-January, 1979-80.

that the easy movement of staff of both language groups can be facilitated, and so that marketing departments working in both languages can be part of head office without problems of "culture shock". Put another way, if a company wishes to operate efficiently all over the country, it is easy to do so in both English and French from Montreal; it is harder to that from Toronto.

Essentially, the notion of "drift" away from Montreal is a handy excuse used by ultra-nationalist politicians in Quebec, as well as by businessmen fleeing from Quebec who do not wish to be subjected to the type of public criticism that was meted out to the Sun Life company. It reached ridiculous extremes when, explaining that their business was expanding in Alberta and British Columbia, an international bank announced that their executive vice-president was, for that reason, moving to . . . Toronto, where he would be nearer to the west than if he stayed in Montreal!

But these ludicrous attempts to blame "westward drift" for Montreal's problems do nothing to help us understand why the real North American trends *from the centre outwards*, to the west, yes, but also towards the east, which are working to the detriment of Cleveland, Buffalo, Detroit and Pittsburgh, and to the benefit of Stamford, New Haven, Boston and Albany, are not working to the detriment of Toronto and to the benefit of Montreal. But co-author Albert's conclusion in the article mentioned earlier is worth repeating:

The factor operating against these trends appears to have started in the early 1960s with the Quiet Revolution. The last year in which gross migration from Ontario to Quebec was greater than the migration the other way was 1961.

While the Quiet Revolution has had only transitory negative effects outside Montreal, comparable to the effects, say, of the Barrett N.D.P. administration in British Columbia, the effects on the English-speaking population of Montreal, in whose hands is concentrated the bulk of the province's private sector, have been deep and continuous. The various pieces of legislation affecting the English language, the violent events of 1970, the present harsh fiscal policy, and the constant questioning of Quebec's constitutional position, have led to a general corporate movement from Montreal, mostly to Toronto.

If, contrary to the "natural" trends, both North American and specifically Canadian, Toronto continues to be built up on the wreckage of Montreal, then, as financier Stephen Jarislowsky said, Quebec politicians "should probably get the Order of Ontario, if there's such a thing. They've been the best city-boosters Toronto has ever had."

Jarislowsky was talking about *Parti Québécois* ministers Jacques Parizeau and Camille Laurin, the tax and language scourges of Montreal's business community; but Ontario's pantheon of heroes should also include statues of Jean Lesage, Daniel Johnson and Robert Bourassa, for the present trend in Quebec is only a continuation of the Quiet Revolution.

The exodus from Montreal has reduced the entire head office industry of that city. A study by W. N. Hall, former President of DOMTAR Ltd, showed that, in 1956, of Canadian companies with controlled assets over $25 million and financial firms with controlled assets over $50 million, those with head offices in Montreal controlled 50 per cent of all Canadian corporate assets, while those in Toronto controlled 31.6 per cent. In 1968, such companies with head offices in Montreal controlled only 38.4 per cent of assets while those in Toronto controlled 38.7 percent.

Other expertise areas are also affected. Montreal was the centre of research and development in engineering with major concentrations of professionals in firms such as Bechtel, S.N.C., Montreal Engineering, Combustion Engineering, and many others, exporting their skills throughout Canada and the world. This, too, is being dissipated. The exodus of engineering companies reflects on employment opportunities for engineering graduates from Montreal's universities. Dr R. E. Bell, then Principal of McGill University, mentioned during the hearings on Bill 101 that McGill's Faculty of Engineering had cancelled a proposed programme in Hydraulics because the managment of Hydro-Québec, the principal local employer of hydraulics engineers, had made it clear that no Anglophone graduates would be encouraged to apply for jobs with that government-owned utility.

During the past few years even the government and its agencies have been saturated with engineers, and with the majority of the principal employers of engineers in the private sector gradually leaving Quebec, young French-Canadian graduates must also leave the province to find employment. The Dean of Engineering at McGill University has stated that very few of his graduates would find employment in Quebec. Where, in 1970, there was strong demand in Quebec for engineers (to the extent that it sought graduates from other provinces and other countries), it is now not only not bringing engineers from elsewhere, it is losing the majority of its engineering graduates, both English and French-speaking.

The pharmaceutical industry was centred in Montreal with 67 per cent of Canada's employment in 1975. This, too is systematically wasting away, and making plans to leave. Where, at one time Montreal was a principal centre of pharmaceutical reasearch and development, the companies, one by one, are reducing or closing their research departments. These departments are normally associated with the research facilities of the universities in Montreal, and the loss of these has reduced job opportunities for those who have completed their post-graduate university programmes; the same problem is seen in the medical field.

The garment industry has been a mainstay of Montreal's economy, with labour-intensive offshoots in nearby towns such as Joliette. Montreal has been one of the fashion centres of the world, employing, in 1975, 200,000 workers, directly or indirectly, in the needle trades. Over the past 20 years creative designs by Montreal clothiers have brought the city into competition with Paris, New York, London and Rome. The industry figures prominently in the list of Quebec's exports of manufactures. As elsewhere, it is in mainly in Jewish hands, and the Jewish community is uneasy about current trends in Quebec. Moreover, the anti-immigrant aspects of Bills 22 and 101 are constricting the supply of labour on which the needle trades depend. There are signs that this industry, too, is becoming uncomfortable in Quebec and is looking elsewhere. A leading men's clothing manufacturer "celebrated" its hundredth anniversary by opening a showroom in Toronto, with one of the two partners moving to that city. It is the standard pattern of the exodus: first one department goes; then a few more join it; then the rest "consolidate" in the new location.

The exodus is beginning to enter the stage of the "vicious circle". As the overt manifestations of discrimination begin to appear, the malaise in the Anglophone communities increases. The most mobile are leaving first. These include creative people in such areas as advertising and marketing. In this group are services such as managment consulting, design and development and research. Once in Toronto it is easy for these experts to fly back to Montreal for a day to do whatever business remains.

The gradual but relentless loss of the expertise section of the economy forces university and technical school graduates to leave Quebec in order to find jobs. A survey of Anglophone junior colleges and universities in January, 1978 showed that 37 per cent of he graduating students were definitely leaving and a further 17 per cent probably leaving. It is interesting that the knowledge of the French language is high in these groups.

Systematic discrimination is being practised in the granting of professional permits and licences in Quebec. Language tests required for licensing in the profession disqualified over 50 per cent of the nursing graduates and large percentages in other professions as well. Over 90 per cent of the graduates in dentistry at McGill University indicated that they would not be entering private practice in Quebec. These figures, disquieting as they may be, are fatal when account is taken of the fact that in-migration of English-speaking people has, for all practical purposes, come to an end.

Even the most menial jobs are unavilable to non-Francophones. After the *péquiste* victory, the new minister, M. Lessard, he of the famous ARRET signs, issued an order to the roads department that no casual employees were to be hired unless they could speak French. Some of those casuals are so-called permanent casuals who work for the roads department every summer, in jobs that recur annually. When a number of these "regulars" presented themselves for work in the summer of 1977 they were summarily refused. Some had been in continuous summer employment with the roads department for 15 and 20 years, working in areas such as Pontiac County or parts of the Gaspé that are predominantly Anglophone. In spite of all entreaties the arrogant racism prevailed. The workers were not re-hired, contradicting assurances by Premier René Lévesque that no Anglophones would lose their jobs because of the regulation.

The public employer has not been the only one to practise race discrimination based on language. Major industries are involved. In some firms that are household names, from brewing to stockbroking, the "Anglophone" functions are being moved out of the province, paring the Montreal administration down to management of the local operation only. Then, as far as feasible, only Francophones are employed in the remaining functions. In other cases, unilingual Anglophones, who happen to be French-Canadian, usually from other provinces, fill certain key jobs. Visiting the manager of a plant one may find that Monsieur Beloit or Monsieur Francoeur hardly speaks French. They have been put in their positions in order to accommodate provincial government officials who use lists of names of senior employees of suppliers as a "quick check" on francization. This ploy can even be worked in reverse; one bank seems to have quite a few managers of branches in central and western Montreal who have English surnames and "neutral" first names, but who are clearly French-Canadian. Presumably, this reassures Anglophone potential new customers, while the government busybodies can be told that bank manager "Ed" McAndrews is "O.K." ("Ed" is really Édouard). This may sound like something out of a novel by John Le Carré, but it is everyday life in a part of Canada!

Francization itself is a mind-shattering concept. During the legislative hearings on Bill 101, civil servants who had been charged with introducing francization under Bill 22 presented a brief. They were then asked to define francization, as the word, in the desired meaning, was not in any dictionary. The answer was that francization was the process whereby something was "made French".

"How" they were asked "do you determine when something is French? . . . Is 'French Onion Soup' French or 'French pastry'? Is it French when the French language is used in the operation of a function? Or is it when the people involved are all French?"

"That would depend on the regulations," they replied.

"If the use of French is required, how do you determine

how much French, and how do you measure the amounts determined?''

Again they answered "This would be determined by the regulations."

It is difficult to imagine in a civilized country like Canada that so much discretionary power has been given to officials to implement a concept that is basically racist. While very little of the effect of this power was felt under Bill 22, because of the delays built into its implementation, francization is now and will prove even more in the future to be one of the most flagrant example of legislated discrimination in existence.

While the direct application of francization has so far been limited, the potential of its application is understood by the business community, and fearing the implications of non-compliance, they are simply avoiding any problems by systematically moving everything essential out of the province, re-establishing in other provinces or in the United States. As the costs of these moves have to be absorbed, they delay normal expansion and instead depreciate outstanding assets, thereby reducing their net tax burden. In effect, the province is not only losing future revenue but also helping to pay for the move through deduction of moving expenses from present taxable profits.

Co-author Shaw recalls a conversation with the president of a major pharmaceutical company. Faced with francization of his industry, which functions internationally in English, and faced also with Federal legislation curtailing the protection of patents on new products, his company made the decision not to proceed with major expansion in Quebec. Worse, the decision was made to move the entire operation out of the province. This decision, taken in 1977, was not being implemented until 1980 when all the newer Quebec facilities have been substantially depreciated. It is costing them millions to make this move, but it is costing Quebec, and Canada, more.

It is not any one aspect of francization, but rather the policy as a whole, that discourages the in-migration of English-speaking managers, experts, and entrepreneurs. Nothing will make a head office move quicker than staff being unwilling to relocate to the head office. The head of one trust company cited not only the difficulty of promoting staff into Montreal, but also the problem of temporarily posting intermediate-level staff outside of head office to gain field experience. After field posting, staff often refuse to return to Montreal head office. Bill 101 and political uncertainty are the usual reasons given for reluctance to move to Montreal. It is difficult to maintain business efficency in these circumstances. The head of one executive recruitment consultancy stated that it is virtually impossible to fill Montreal vacancies — that in 85 to 90 per cent of cases it is not even possible to move past the statement that the location is Montreal. The refusal is immediate.

Greater Montreal has a population of 2.7 million, of which 1.7 million are French-Canadian. The private sector of Montreal (plus Crown Corporations, but not counting Civil Service or hospitals or education) provides about 750,000 jobs. This private sector is 65 per cent non-Francophone in terms of management and ownership. They are people who almost without exception oppose ultra-nationalism. Consequently, it stands to reason that the exodus has only just begun. We cannot rule out the possibility of Montreal becoming an economic Hiroshima. The tragedy is that while the "crisis" of national unity and the harm being done to Canada as a whole can be overcome, the people, the head offices, company divisions, and entire companies in some cases, are not going to come back.

11

The "Hand in the Cookie Jar"

The overwhelming majority of French-Canadians in Quebec sense that what is happening in Quebec today is wrong. It is like the boy caught with his hand in the cookie jar. He knows he is doing wrong. Yet, he would like to get at the cookie just the same. Quebec's political leadership is like that. They know that legislation like Bill 101 is wrong. Nevertheless they enjoy the political advantages that such legislation provides, and are therefore unlikely to change or repeal these iniquitous laws.

The Federal Liberal party likewise benefits by giving its indirect blessing to these laws. The criticism Pierre-Elliott Trudeau offered of Bill 22 was that it was "stupid". That is typical of the hypocritical politician who tries to gain support from both the proponents and the opponents of anything controversial by implying to the one that, while they had a good idea, they were not clever enough in putting it into effect, and implying to the others that their opposition to the basic principle is shared by the politician.

At some level of consciousness, at least in Montreal, the French-Canadian people know that the language laws must be removed before any significant change will be visible in the social and economic climate. At the same time they are savouring a period of preferential advantage in employment and in the unquestioned acceptance of francization. They are also conscious of the benefits of state intervention and discriminatory policies in government purchasing and contracting. It is therefore hard to balance justice and fair play, or longer-term benefits, against the immediate advantages of discriminatory policies. One often hears the remark "It will never be the way it was." It is also important that it not remain the way it is.

French Quebec cannot go on ignoring the growing awareness abroad of what is going on in the province, and the accusations of racism in the international press. An international symposium on racism was held in Montreal in 1978. It was not amazing in the present climate of Quebec that such key participants as Yvon Charbonneau, then president of the militant Quebec teachers' union (C.E.Q.) and Michel Chartrand, of the Montreal construction workers' union, decried apartheid in South Africa while at the same time lending outspoken support to the language legislation at home!

The radicals are not the only ones who wish to retain discriminatory language legislation. Both Rodrigue Biron, former leader of the *Union Nationale*, and Claude Ryan, leader of the Quebec Liberal Party, are in favour of keeping most of the features of Bill 101. In this, they are even outdone by such a Federal luminary as Max Yalden, Commissioner of Official Languages, who echoed Camille Laurin's intention of "increasing that which is French and *even diminishing that which is English.*"[1] Yalden said of francization *"How far it is . . . necessary to repress the use, display and acquisition of English . . . is another matter."*[2] All seem prepared to make some changes to allow Anglophones from outside Quebec to enrol their children in English schools, and to allow bilingual signs, but few other changes. All wish to keep francization as a policy despite the negative economic effects.

French Quebeckers are at least a little concerned about their image, but not yet ready to improve it. When an Italian journalist wrote in his Milan newspaper that the *Parti Québécois* was fascist and racist there was pressure by both the Federal and Quebec governments to refute the report. René Lévesque went so far as to write a personal letter to the Pope denying any racist tendency on the part of his government.

Lévesque frequently travels abroad, ready to defend the actions of his government by saying that only those steps necessary to protect the French language are being taken. But foreign journalists who have taken the trouble to visit Quebec are critical. There is growing international concern about Quebec's treatment of its immigrants. In such countries as Greece, Italy, Portugal, and Germany the word has reached the media — that new immigrants are treated differently in Quebec from anywhere else in the New World. Stories of clandestine schools, the intimidation of small children through language tests, and the arrogance of government language officials have

---

[1] Interview in *Ici Québec* magazine, March, 1978.
[2] Annual Report for 1978, p. 32. (our italics — W.F.S.& L.A.)

deterred their citizens from emigrating to Quebec. This negative image of Quebec has also affected the tourist industry. The hotelkeepers of Montreal, already burdened by an oversupply of rooms, high municipal taxes, and one of the highest minimum wages in North America, are very much aware that visitors who had always preferred Montreal and Quebec City to Toronto or the Maritimes, are now holidaying in English-speaking Canada as the anti-English-language hostility in the province becomes common knowledge. Quebec City especially feels the backlash. Always a year-round tourist attraction, the city has found its volume of visitors dropping at an alarming rate. There was a full one-third drop in attendance in 1978 at the Winter Carnival. The drop in the number of visitors from the rest of Canada and the United States was thought to be 70 per cent.

Until 1975, there was much sympathy for French Canada as a collectivity trying to protect its language against the pressure of a North American English-speaking population of 250 million. There was recognition that the French language and culture deserved a status equal to that of English. There was a positive tourist image as people came to Quebec to see the "difference". But tourists are not as myopic as some ultra-nationalists believe. They can sense when a friendly atmosphere is bogus, and they avoid places that are subject to moods of hostility, hatred and especially racism.

Since Bill 22, the world has become aware that Quebec wants to be recognized as different, but that it refuses to recognize English-speaking rights in Quebec.

Some of the media outside Quebec, such as *Saturday Night* magazine and the Toronto *Globe & Mail*, have tried to downplay the impact of Bill 101 but, increasingly, both individuals and businesses are learning that Bill 22 was, and Bill 101 is, every bit as bad as their most rabid opponents say they are.

When we see signs in French in other provinces and even in New England and Florida, only to find that, in Quebec, English signs are "illegal", as is the Hebrew sign for the Kosher butcher and the ideographic words for the Chinese restaurant, it is evident that something is wrong. When Anglophone nursing graduates were unable to practise their profession in Quebec, and it became known outside the province,

English Words Obliterated, Montreal, 1980. (Only one third are Francophones in this district.)

teams of recruiters came to Montreal from Florida, Texas and California to interview these girls for purposes of employment. The abuses of Bills 22 and 101 and the French Language Board are common knowledge to potential employers throughout the continent.

French-Canadians are concerned. It is because of this that the small businessman of Quebec is particularly hostile to the *Parti Québécois*. He feels the deterioration of the business climate around him, and the growing hostility from Anglophones outside the province. He knows that Lévesque and the *Péquistes* must be removed at all costs. Yet he ignores the issue of language laws, feeling that as long as referendums are defeated and Lévesque removed from power, all will be rosy again.

This attitude was typified by the *Conseil du Patronat*, which reflects the views of Francophone businessmen, in a 1978 brief to Réne Lévesque. The emphasis was on the need for a quick referendum with a clear question in order to erase the uncertainty. They paid lip service to the abuses of Bill 101, seemingly burying their heads in the sand to avoid facing the disastrous effects of the legislation on all levels of business activity in Montreal, which is the tax milch cow of the province. Individually the businessmen recognize the damage. Collectively it is unacceptable for French-Canadians to criticize the language legislation.

The obvious damage caused by the language laws is the loss of businesses but the hidden damage caused by lost opportunity is even greater. Francization is really crippling the French-Canadians in their quest for economic power. Francization means, not protecting that which is now French, but making French that which is not now French; in other words trying to turn English-speaking firms into French ones. That is why the refusal by Roger Lemelin, Publisher of the respected French-language newspaper *La Presse*, to apply for a "Certificate of Francization" was of great symbolic importance. It was Lemelin's way of showing that francization is saying 'All right you English, Jews, Greeks and Italians, jump into the marketplace and swim with the sharks and the crocodiles. If you succeed, then you must give us 80 per cent of the top jobs because you happen to be doing business in Quebec.'

Under francization, the bright, ambitious French-Canadians

who should be starting their own businesses or joining small but growing Francophone firms are accepting the "plum" jobs with fancy titles and perquisites that are being handed out by the big Anglophone companies. Some Anglophone business-men have told us that this has its "plus" side — that young French-Canadians who have been catapulted into senior posi-tions at least have the opportunity to observe the workings of business, and to appreciate the concerns of top managers with such indicators as daily cash balances, profit and loss, and the balance sheet; in other words, the "bottom line". The hope is that these French-Canadians will somehow act as a transmission belt to French Quebec public opinion so that the political and social climate for business will improve.

Of course, these young Francophone executives are learn-ing the very opposite. They are learning that the way to "suc-ceed in business without really trying" is to support franciza-tion. The accommodating attitude of English Montreal beckons French-Canadians into a blind alley. Even such mundane gestures by Anglophones as trying to do their shopping in French only misleads the French. One young Francophone business school student said "I worked in a store in Beaconsfield. I was very surprised how hard the Anglophones were trying to speak French. Even there."[3] The first thing that a young business student should learn about working in a store is that the store is there to please the customer. Instead, they are being given the idea that the customer is there to please them!

The evidence that francization is crippling French-Canadian enterprise in Montreal lies in the fact that Francophone enterprise is flourishing in the "Miracles" of the Beauce, Lake St John, Abitibi and other remote regions where, for the first time, French-Canadians are doing everything for themselves, using their own savings and their own credit, in their own special way and not copying the "English" or American ways — and succeeding in the modern, competitive North American marketplace; right in there with the sharks and the crocodiles! An example is "Ray Jeans", whose turnover is in the tens of millions, owned and operated by Raymond Boisvert, and penetrating one of the most competitive markets in North

---

[3] Interview by James Quig, *The Gazette*, December 8, 1979.

America. (Boisvert is a canny man. He even ran as P.Q.
candidate in a by-election in 1979 — preaching renewed
Federalism!)

But there is no "Miracle" in Montreal.[4] Why not?
Because, in the remote regions, where there are no Anglophone firms to francize, the locals use their own initiative; in
Montreal, the Anglophone businessmen, instead of telling
young Francophones literally "Mind your own business!"
foolishly heed the advice of Pierre Laurin, head of the H.E.C.
business school, who "started knocking on *anglais* doors, telling potential employers about his school and his graduates. . .
What mattered was that his boys weren't getting hired by the
big English companies. . . . Too many ended up working for the
provincial government. Too few joined large English-speaking
corporations."[5]

---

[4] For some time, readers of the Toronto press have been regaled with
enthusiastic articles about the new spirit of enterprise in French Montreal.
Full "credit" is given to to Bill 101 despite the obvious contradiction that
prompts the question, 'Why try to turn the English firms into French if
you are enterprising enough to start your own?' In any case it turns out
that the few examples cited are kept alive by government. Anderson
Charters, (*Financial Post*, December 8, 1979), described "an agressive,
young consulting company, S— — Inc. . . . that practises the en-
trepreneurial principle . . . S— —'s clients are as varied as the subjects it
has tackled. It includes *the Federal and Quebec governments, the gamut of
public policy research institutes,* and a mix of companies from the private
sector." — Ah, the reader might say, that last indicates that S— — has
jumped into the marketplace, after all. Sorry, the "private sector" turns
out to be something else. "Often we are hired by private enterprise *to
study the effect a public policy problem will have on it.*" (our italics —
W.F.S.& L.A.) S— —, profiting from Bill 101, "also has been closely
involved with language legislation, drafting francization of business documents." S— — is not the only service firm to batten on government; the
advertising agencies, having lost commercial business because of the
exodus, take in hundreds of thousands of dollars in Quebec government
service advertising. The province is plastered with billboards promoting
wholesome diets, moderation in drink and other "motherhood" themes.
It is the ultra-nationalists' way of keeping an army of talented people on
their payroll. They crowd the fashionable bars in Montreal, creating a
kind of "Potemkin village" atmosphere of activity to impress the uniniti-
ate. Vancouver columnist Allan Fotheringham swallowed this, "hook, line
and sinker", on a 1979 visit to Montreal, when he concluded that the
'new French crowd' encountered in the Ritz-Carlton Hotel was the rep-
lacement for the departing Anglophones.

[5] Paraphrased by James Quig, *The Gazette*, December 8, 1979.

With all goodwill, we believe that this attitude, on which Professor Laurin has been dining out for years, bespeaks the same deep-rooted "Inferiority Complex" that weighs down on his older brother Camille Laurin. While not denying that Montreal's Anglophone businesses can teach young French-Canadians some of the "nuts and bolts" of particular branches of industry, we believe that the "Miracle" of French-speaking business in Montreal, which has tremendous potential, will only come about when the French go into business for themselves. Professor Laurin did at least have the good sense to invite Professor Nathan Glazer of the Harvard Business School to come to the H.E.C. and say "We would all hope to see . . . success in the economic sphere. But this requires not . . . using political muscle to advance economically, but the difficult road of improving the economic capacity of the Francophone majority."[6]

Even the short-term benefits of francization are already proving to be ephemeral. The Positive Action report of June, 1979, shows that, in Montreal establishments with over 200 employees, while the proportion of Francophones in head-office-type positions rose from 30.0 per cent in 1972 to 34.1 per cent in 1977 to 35.7 per cent in 1978-79, the total number of those jobs, which had stopped growing (having gone from 71,130 to 71,101 in the first period), declined sharply to 65,040 in 1978-79. The result is that the number of Francophones in head-office-type jobs in those large establishments actually *declined* from 24,255 in 1977 to 23,194 in 1978-79. The exodus wins.

Part of the problem is the naive belief in the benefits of higher education. In the 1960s, ultra-nationalists organized quite hostile demonstrations in front of McGill University under the slogan *McGill français!* It was thought that the English dominated Montreal because of what they learned, or whom they met, at that institution. While both of us are proud graduates of McGill, and would not wish to denigrate the value of its teaching, the fact is that, in essence, the only place to learn about business is the marketplace. But the blind belief in education dies hard. For sheer imbecility on this subject, no one

---

[6] Paper delivered at a symposium at the École des Hautes Études Commerciales, May 16, 1978.

can exceed Bernard Landry, Lévesque's senior Economics minister. Asked if the "Miracles" in the remote regions could be credited to the Quiet Revolution, he said "The influence of the Quiet Revolution, of course, can be seen in the newly booming economies of the remote areas of Quebec. Actually, where the action is in Quebec is La Beauce, Abitibi, Lac St-Jean, Rimouski, Matane, Mont Joli, and so on. . . . the rest of the province is now leading Montreal. And this is a direct consequence of the Quiet Revolution. There are universities now in outlying locations, the standard of education is a lot higher . . ."[7] Maybe Landry believes that Raymond Boisvert, the jeans king of the Beauce, obtained a Ph.D. in "Trouser Technology"! In fact, Boisvert learned the "nuts and bolts" of the business in the hurly-burly of Montreal's needle trades; and the Perron brothers' father started their woods business hauling logs on contract for a big pulp and paper company, using horses! (Messrs Boisvert and Perron may of course have attended excellent schools and universities, but that has little bearing on their successes or failures in business.)

So all the nastiness of Bill 22 and Bill 101 brings little benefit to French Quebec, other than to appeal to a certain spirit of what can best be described as "playful vengefulness" — enjoying the amazing sight of *English* signs being taken down — though not seriously wishing to bully the minority. But the poor image continues to surface. French Quebeckers travelling outside the province are finding it increasingly difficult to explain the actions of their government. They now resort to blaming the *Parti Québécois* radicals. Five years earlier they would have given a long and convincing story of the need to redress a long list of past injustices.

Bills 22 and 101 are bad news for Francophones outside Quebec. By and large French-Canadians and Acadians in the other provinces looked to Quebec to provide an element of leadership for a better future throughout Canada. They no longer look to Quebec with confidence, but rather with apprehension. Great progress has been made by non-Quebec Francophones. They do not wish that progress to be compromised.

---

[7] Interview with Dalton Robertson, *Financial Post*, December 8, 1979.

That is why we compare the situation in Quebec to the boy caught with his hand in the cookie jar. French-Canadians know that what Quebec is doing is wrong. They must now realize that they cannot take the cookie and stop being wrong. On the other hand they do not want to retract and lose all they have gained. That is understandable.

Thus the great problem for French Canada is to retain the gains that it has made while establishing the open society vital to their economic, social and political health. Knowing that the pendulum has swung too far, they fear that, in swinging back, it could well destroy the progress of the past 20 years. That too is understandable.

How much this swing accelerates depends on the widening polarization between English and French Canada. French-Canadians must realize that legislation directed against the English language is ultimately a serious threat to their own language rather than the great protector that it pretends to be. That is the challenge for French-Canadians.

Every society has its bias and discrimination, but Canada, perhaps because of its vastness, perhaps because of its harsh environment, has measured its discrimination to an acceptable degree. Perhaps that is why we are regarded by other nations as relatively open. God knows that we have bigots, but the vast majority of our people understand the importance of toleration, if not of goodwill. Unilingual French-Canadians report that visiting Toronto is like visiting a foreign country. But it is equally true of an Eskimo from Aklavik, or a Newfoundlander from Come-by-Chance. For that matter, a Torontonian visiting Quebec City feels a different atmosphere. There is nothing unusual in this. Canada, because of its vast size and its multitude of social ingredients, has more different groups than any nation per capita in the world, and that is remarkable when one compares the differences within the Soviet Union or the United States.

We must begin, however, by saying that this country is indivisible. The geopolitical integrity of Canada is not negotiable. Then we must sit down together, and discuss our problems in order to solve them with justice and equity. We can meet this challenge only if no group demands a special deal before the negotiations start. Quebec abuses our political system when it insists on such a deal. Quebec's trump card is the threat of separation. The threat of separation is a totally unrealistic advantage, but the Quebec government has convinced the rest of the country that it holds this card. Despite all the political gymnastics of the past 10 years, it does not.

12

The Fever Will Break

We have described the resolution of French Canada's "Inferiority Complex" as a kind of passage through a fever. When a weak, sickly patient goes through such a crisis he utters a few feeble moans, and his highest temperature may be 103°. But when a strong, healthy, young bull of a man goes through such a crisis he bellows loudly. When the peak temperature reaches 105° the orderlies have to be called in. So it is with French Canada — basically, a lusty and vigorous young man whose fever-crisis is worrying his friends and relations.

They need not worry. Already the signs of returning health, of the disappearance of the "Inferiority Complex" are present, even while the "crisis" of separatism is rampaging. The brothers Perron of La Sarre broke the $100 million barrier in their 1979 turnover. When interviewed, their talk is all about plywood, waterboard, and PROFITS.[1] Gilles Villeneuve expects to break new records in the world of car racing. Pierre Péladeau is planning his next foray into the American tabloid newspaper market.

More and more, English-speaking Canadians are becoming accustomed to reading of French-Canadian successes. Gilles Villeneuve and the brothers Perron are only a forerunner of many French-Canadian successes to come. At first, English-speaking Canadians may feel uncomfortable; they are not used to seeing so many French names among Canadian winners in any endeavour, national or international. But gradually they will get used to, then come to like, and eventually share with French-Canadians the pride in the fact that one of *our* boys, or girls, has won.

---

[1] But "Jean Perron warned that his company's expansion is being held back because of its inability to obtain bilingual personnel, meaning French Canadians who speak English." — report from the annual conference of the Association of M.B.A.s of Quebec — *Financial Post*, December 12, 1979.

And what about the French-Canadians? They will come to realize that their achievements are their own; that they owe nothing to any politician; that the "Quiet Revolution", while it brought some needed changes, is basically a politicians' trophy; that the era of inferiority, when French-Canadians relied on politics for advancement, is over; that the prophets of separatism are the bogey-men of the everlasting "Inferiority Complex"; that they don't need the constricting baggage of the Crown Corporations and the Bill 101s; and that their achievements are not so few and far between that they have to be hoarded under the fake name "Québécois", but are so bountiful that they can safely run the risk of being diluted with all the other Canadians.

The separatists are wrong when they assert that it is fear of independence that motivates their opponents. The fear expressed by the opponents of separatism is the fear of being cut off from the larger opportunities of Canada. It is the separatists who preach fear — fear that their people cannot walk without government crutches; fear that their language cannot survive.

We are optimistic about the future. We have no doubt that the social and political situation will change for the better. The only question is how long; and how much damage will have been done. How long will it take to repair the damage both to the image and character of Quebec, and the image and character of Canada as a whole?

Canadians outside Quebec find it difficult to accept the double standard upheld by their Federal government. The question is changing from "What does Quebec want?" to "Let them go, and good riddance." There is no doubt that, discounting for "redneck" prejudices, morale in the Federal Civil Service, Crown Corporations and in the Canadian Armed Forces has been hurt by discrimination against non-Francophones to enhance the French Fact. The rest of Canada sees compulsory bilingualism in product packaging and institutional signs, while the ultra-nationalists insist on unilingualism in Quebec. Thousands of former Quebeckers live all over Canada, each of whom feels an attachment to his native province. These people know what is happening to their relations and friends in Quebec, and they are increasingly resentful.

The introduction of Bill 22 in 1974 raised the eyebrows of

English-speaking Canadians in other provinces, and made it difficult for head offices to transfer personnel to Montreal. But its full impact was not then understood. When Bill 101, the P.Q.'s French language charter, was enacted, a deeper reaction set in. With the threat of separation poised over them, the majority of Canadians, unaware of the concept of that law, reassured themselves that Pierre-Elliott Trudeau was the man who could handle René Lévesque, and that somehow any abuses arising from that law would be stopped. But the abuses did not stop and slowly and inexorably Trudeau's image as the cure for the problem changed into Trudeau's image as the cause of the problem. The polarization has gained momentum. It is this polarization, and Quebec's deteriorating image, that calls for correction. When correction begins, the threat of separation will assume a more realistic low profile.

The false assumption by Quebec leaders that Bills 22 or 101 could be enacted without acute polarization is a tragedy in itself. However, it demonstrated a great truth. North American society does not lightly accept any restrictions on individual rights, and where, in Canada, the reaction may have been slow, it is accelerating. To decelerate it will require a major change in the general attitude of Quebec's public leaders.

There are those who suggest that the problem will be resolved once Quebeckers have had an opportunity to express themselves in a referendum. "Once we have been able to demonstrate that we are overwhelmingly committed to staying in Canada" they suggest "the uncertainty will end and prosperity will return." "Its not language" say some "its economics." "Once we have made the constitutional changes that all of Canada wants, the threat will disappear." These statements are seen in all the media. They are a. hope that simple solutions will reverse the polarization already generated; that the "English" will be able to live with the language legislation . . . that it is a matter of time, and that language law is not a factor in Montreal's economic difficulties and the resultant squeeze on Quebec's tax revenues. We do not agree. Language law is the key cause of Montreal's decline; it is what has brought about the reversal of the Quiet Revolution's once positive reputation in Canada; and it is the principal cause of polarization.

Our long-term hope is that separation will become to the

Parti Québécois what "funny money" became for the Social Credit parties of Canada's far west — a half-forgotten relic.

Nevertheless, referendums will continue to be used as threatening instruments, with first, the Federal government, and then other provinces such as Alberta, getting into the act. No matter what the question, each referendum is perceived as being the question For or Against a province remaining part of Canada. Thus the appearance of a referendum question, and the threat that it poses, are more important than the content of the question itself. Regardless of the question, the result is regarded by most Canadians as the separatist option versus the Federalist option.

In no way is the holding of referendums of any value. The day after a "No" result may be a day of jubilation, but it does not solve any problem. Nor does a "Yes" vote. It is interesting that Fabien Roy, National Leader of the Social Credit party, suggests that he would vote "Yes" in a referendum because a separatist result would precipitate negotiations on constitutional review, while a Federalist result would only begin the debate all over again. One could almost accept his proposal except for the volatile emotions that such referendums generate.

Referendums will not solve any of Quebec's problems. They only serve to deepen polarization within Canada. The need is for Quebec and the other provinces to recognize the need to live in harmony, respecting the French Fact, in Canada Federally and in those provinces that have a French Fact, and the English Fact in Quebec. Before this can happen, the accelerating polarization must be reversed so that fundamentally positive attitudes may surface again.

Defeating the *Parti Québécois* and replacing it with another party, unprepared to make major changes, would be fruitless. Replacing René Lévesque with a surrogate Robert Bourassa could do serious damage. Those who waited out the P.Q. régime would become discouraged, and the exodus would accelerate.

Quebec has three choices. It can underline or simply maintain its ultra-nationalism with a continuing degradation of its social and political climate. The exodus would continue and accelerate, state intervention to compensate would grow, the eroding tax base would become overloaded, and Quebec would become progressively more isolated from the main stream of the North American economy; a kind of Mexico.

The polarization associated with this choice would make the rest of Canada more anti-French, with increased pressure to assimilate Francophones outside Quebec. This factor, together with the increased out-migration of French Quebeckers in search of employment, would undermine the French language base. The pendulum would swing within a Montreal denuded of its active English-speaking population, towards a kind of "Cardiffization"[2] of the city, further undermining the French base. The devaluation of self, engendered by the relative drop in standard of living and the exodus of youth, would perpetuate the "Inferiority Complex".

The second course that Quebec could follow is one of a slow recovery occasioned by an attempt by the leadership to continue its "French-only" policy, while making modest concessions to minorities. This course too would move Quebec out of the North American main stream, but allow some growth. Time would work to bring about an economic recovery. But the process could last half a century, and would not help Montreal which, by the census of 2011, might only be Canada's 7th-largest city.[3]

---

[2] Cardiff, with South Wales generally, which is to Wales what Montreal is to Quebec, is staunchly Welsh in makeup and sentiment, but the people insist on using the English language exclusively; the Welsh language is only a relic there. The rest of Wales is still basically a Welsh mother-tongue region, where children learn English only as a second language. (See also *Only language zones will save French in urban districts*, by co-author Albert, *The Gazette*, October 18, 1979.)

[3] Here is our guess, based on the two premises that francization will continue to be imposed on Montreal, and that Ottawa will continue as a bilingual city (overtaking Toronto as the refuge for Montreal business) with many Francophones working in Ottawa but living in Hull: Population in 2011:

1. Toronto-Hamilton		4,600,000
2. Ottawa-Hull		2,500,000
3. Vancouver		2,400,000
4. Calgary		1,900,000
5. Winnipeg		1,800,000
6. Edmonton		1,300,000
7. Montreal		1,000,000

The last figure accords with an unpublished study made by Professor Donald Armstrong of McGill University's Faculty of Management, based on earlier research by W. N. Hall. In correlating size of largest city with

The third course, the best and most probable, is to accept The North American Challenge, with Montreal as the arena.

Montreal, while again becoming the city where ambitious men become millionaires, but this time with the French participating along with the English, would probably still be a city of two solitudes, but those two solitudes would be closer, because there would be greater and more genuine respect for the French, because of their achievements.

Just as the English-speaking would learn genuine respect for the French, the French-Canadians would learn to extend a genuine welcome to the unilingual English; not a welcome based on fear of losing a job or a sale, nor on inferiority, but an open welcome based on the respect between equals — yet where one has accepted the fact that North America speaks English, and is content in that acceptance.

With such an attitude Montreal would once more be the pivot of Canada, which would become a truly great country and not just the map of a richly-endowed section of Earth's surface. Quebec is now, and long has been, an integral part of North America. It must recognize this truth. It can and should retain its French character. At the same time it must be an open society that, in being different, tolerates difference. The rest of Canada must accept this difference, and it will. But the threats must stop.

---

size of country, for advanced countries of under 10 million population, and comparing them to Quebec, Montreal turns out to reach a peak size at about one million, based on Quebec's present population. (Since Quebec would lose most of its Anglophone population under continued francization, the figure of one million would still apply in 2011.) When the largest city is not the capital (e.g. Auckland, New Zealand or Zurich, Switzerland), the feasible ratio to total population is even lower.

BIBLIOGRAPHY

A. Aspinall (Edited by): *The Later Correspondence of George III*, Vol. 1, Cambridge (Eng.), The Cambridge University Press, 1962

Jacques Brossard: *L'accession à la souveraineté et le cas du Québec*, Montreal, Les Presses de l'Université de Montréal, 1976

Lawrence J. Burpee: *An Historical Atlas of Canada*, Toronto, Thomas Nelson & Sons (Canada) Ltd, 1927

J.M.S. Careless: *The Union of the Canadas*, Toronto, McClelland and Stewart Limited, 1967

Jean-Pierre Charbonneau and Gilbert Paquette: *L'Option*, Montreal, Les Éditions de l'Homme, 1978

Edgar A. Collard: *Montreal: The Days That Are No More*, Toronto, Doubleday Canada Limited, 1976

Commission d'étude sur l'intégrité du territoire du Québec: *La frontière du Labrador*, Vol. 3.1, Quebec City, Service de la réprographie, 1973; also *Les frontières méridionales*, Vol. 6.1, 1971

Samuel Adams Drake: *The Border Wars of New England*, (Charles Scribner's Sons, 1897), reprinted, Williamstown, Mass., Corner House Publishers, 1973

Emerson D. Fite and Archibald Freeman: *A Book of Old Maps*, (Harvard University Press, 1926), reprinted, New York, Arno Press, 1969

Denis Héroux, Robert Lahaise, and Noel Vallerand: *La Nouvelle France*, Montreal, Centre de psychologie et de pédagogie, 1967

House of Commons (England): *Copy or Extracts of Correspondence between the Colonial Office, the Government of the Canadian Dominion, and the Hudson's Bay Company, relating to the Surrender of Rupert's Land by the Hudson's Bay Company, and for the Admission thereof into the Dominion of Canada*, London, 1869.

Bruce Hutchison: *The Struggle for the Border*, Toronto, Longmans, Green & Company, 1955

Richard J. Joy: *Languages in Conflict*, Ottawa (P.O. Box 2402, Station D), the Author, 1967

Legislative Assembly of the Province of Quebec: *Sessional Papers*, Quebec City, (no imprint), 1895, 1896, 1897, 1898.

D. H. Miller-Barstow: *Beatty of the C.P.R.*, Toronto, McClelland and Stewart Limited, 1951

Ministère des Terres et Forêts: *Répertoire des cantons*, Quebec City, 1974

Elain Allan Mitchell: *Fort Timiskaming and the Fur Trade*, Toronto, University of Toronto Press, 1977

W. L. Morton: *The Critical Years*, Toronto, McClelland and Stewart Limited, 1964

Hilda Neatby: *Quebec, The Revolutionary Age*, Toronto, McClelland and Stewart Limited, 1966

Jean Provencher: *René Lévesque - Portrait of a Québécois*, Toronto, Gage Publishing Limited, 1975 (translated by David Ellis); originally: *René Lévesque: portrait d'un Québécois*, Montreal, Les Éditions La Presse, 1974

Stuart E. Rosenberg: *The Jewish Community in Canada*, Vol. 1, Toronto/Montreal, McClelland and Stewart Limited, 1970

Max Savelle: *The Diplomatic History of the Canadian Boundary, 1749-1763*, New Haven, Yale University Press, 1940

Robert Sellar: *The History of the County of Huntingdon*, Huntingdon, P.Q., *The Gleaner*, 1888, reprinted 1975

Adam Shortt and Arthur G. Doughty (Selected and Edited by): *Documents relating to The Constitutional History of Canada, 1759-1791*, Vol. 1, Ottawa, The King's Printer, 1918.

Marcel Trudel: *Atlas Historique du Canada français*, Quebec City, Les Presses de l'Université Laval, 1961.

INDEX

204